Building Peace After War

Mats Berdal

Building Peace After War

Mats Berdal

IISS The International Institute for Strategic Studies

The International Institute for Strategic Studies

Arundel House | 13–15 Arundel Street | Temple Place | London | WC2R 3DX | UK

First published October 2009 by **Routledge**
4 Park Square, Milton Park, Abingdon, Oxon, OX14 4RN

for **The International Institute for Strategic Studies**
Arundel House, 13–15 Arundel Street, Temple Place, London, WC2R 3DX, UK
www.iiss.org

Simultaneously published in the USA and Canada by **Routledge**
270 Madison Ave., New York, NY 10016

Routledge is an imprint of Taylor & Francis, an Informa Business

© 2009 The International Institute for Strategic Studies

DIRECTOR-GENERAL AND CHIEF EXECUTIVE John Chipman
EDITOR Tim Huxley
MANAGER FOR EDITORIAL SERVICES Ayse Abdullah
ASSISTANT EDITOR Katharine Fletcher
COVER/PRODUCTION John Buck

The International Institute for Strategic Studies is an independent centre for research, information and debate on the problems of conflict, however caused, that have, or potentially have, an important military content. The Council and Staff of the Institute are international and its membership is drawn from almost 100 countries. The Institute is independent and it alone decides what activities to conduct. It owes no allegiance to any government, any group of governments or any political or other organisation. The IISS stresses rigorous research with a forward-looking policy orientation and places particular emphasis on bringing new perspectives to the strategic debate.

The Institute's publications are designed to meet the needs of a wider audience than its own membership and are available on subscription, by mail order and in good bookshops. Further details at www.iiss.org.

Printed and bound in Great Britain by Bell & Bain Ltd, Thornliebank, Glasgow

British Library Cataloguing in Publication Data
A catalogue record for this book is available from the British Library

Library of Congress Cataloging in Publication Data

ISBN 978-0-415-47436-8
ISSN 0567-932X

ADELPHI 407

To Dominique Jacquin-Berdal

1966–2006

ACKNOWLEDGEMENTS

A number of people have read and commented on all or parts of this book in draft form. Others, some of whom wish to remain anonymous, agreed to be interviewed or, more informally, to share background information and personal observations. I am particularly grateful to Karen Ballentine, Mark Bishop, Michael J. Boyle, Matt Bryden, James Cockayne, David Keen, Antonio Giustozzi, Kieran Mitton, Funmi Olonisakin, Timothy Raeymaekers, Tor Tanke-Holm, Dominik Zaum, David Ucko and Nader Mousavizadeh. The book is dedicated with love, affection and a profound and ineradicable sense of loss to Dominique Jacquin-Berdal. Her subtlety as a thinker about international relations, her plain common sense and distrust of conventional wisdom have, hopefully, rubbed off on the author and left some traces in the pages that follow.

An early draft of sections of the book was presented at a conference organised by the Norwegian Institute for Defence Studies in April 2007. The proceedings of that conference were published in John Andreas Olsen (ed), *On New Wars* (Oslo: Norwegian Institute for Defence Studies, 2007). A shorter version of Chapter 3, since substantially revised, appeared as 'The UN Peacebuilding Commission: The Rise and Fall of a Good Idea' in Michael Pugh, Neil Cooper and Mandy Turner (eds), *Critical Perspectives on War-transformed Economies* (Basingstoke: Palgrave, 2008). Finally, I wish to thank the Rockefeller Foundation for funding much of the research on which the book is based.

Contents

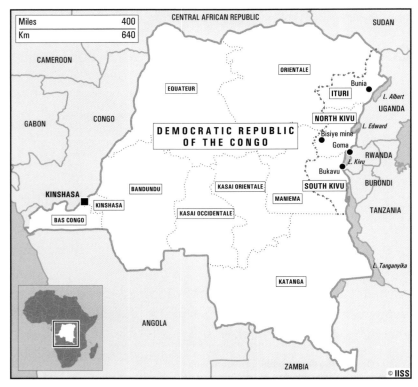

The Democratic Republic of the Congo

INTRODUCTION

Any attempt to step back and survey the post-Cold War period as a whole – to single out features that set it aside from earlier eras in the history of modern international relations – would surely reveal, as one of its most striking characteristics, the widespread practice of external intervention undertaken with the express aim of building 'sustainable peace' within societies ravaged by war and violent conflict.

Such 'post-conflict' interventions have, it is true, taken a variety of forms and have involved different constellations of actors, institutional sponsors and sources of legitimising authority. They have differed sharply in terms of political context and in the degree to which local populations and elites have embraced the foreign presence. In Kosovo, Afghanistan and Iraq, efforts to consolidate peace came in the wake of major hostilities initiated and led by Western powers. In Cambodia and Bosnia-Herzegovina, they followed the entry into force of ambitious, though still fragile and tenuous, internationally sponsored peace agreements. In yet another set of circumstances, they have grown out of what were initially more limited peace-keeping endeavours, as in the cases of Angola, Liberia, Sierra

Leone and the Democratic Republic of the Congo (DRC). The intensity of the commitment of the intervening authority has also varied greatly, from skeletal provision for election and human-rights monitoring in Central America in the early 1990s to fully fledged governance over large swathes of territory, as in Timor Leste and Kosovo. The practice has also been highly selective.[1] Since the mid 1990s the Balkans have often been described, not without justification, as one large 'peacebuilding laboratory'.[2] From March 1992 to September 1993, a major UN mission – at the time, the most ambitious field operation in the history of the organisation – deployed to Cambodia with a mandate that spanned human-rights protection, refugee repatriation, the organisation of elections and economic reconstruction. Haiti has been host to no fewer than four UN missions since the threat of an American invasion forced the removal from power of the military junta led by General Raoul Cédras in September 1994. In contrast to these major commitments of time, resources and personnel, other regions and countries have received far less, if any, attention. For a long time one glaring example of neglect and selectivity was Burundi, a country where 'several hundred thousand people' are believed to have perished in 'bloody cycles of violence and reprisal' in the years between the murder of the country's president, Melchior Ndadaye, in 1993 and the arrival of a major UN operation in June 2004.[3]

When the UN eventually did deploy to Burundi, however, with a mission that at one point numbered some 6,000 military and civilian personnel, it assumed many of the new and more ambitious tasks that have become a feature of the organisation's post-Cold War activity, including human-rights monitoring, the disarmament, demobilisation and reintegration (DDR) of soldiers, and security-sector reform. That very fact, in the context of the argument made here, is significant. For while the differences between the types of operation outlined above are unquestionably important, common to the post-Cold War interventions that form the subject of this book is nonetheless a level of ambition that is qualitatively different from that of UN field operations during the Cold War. Nor, it may be added, is there much in the history of the League of Nations – an organisation whose innovative aspects and activities, especially in the 1920s, have tended to be overshadowed by its ultimate demise – to compare in scale and ambition with the post-Cold War international commitment to re-engineer and reshape societies by means of an external presence.[4] For all their under-acknowledged variety, UN peacekeeping activities during the Cold War were limited, albeit with some significant exceptions, to the mitigation and containment of violent conflict. As a general rule, they involved the deployment of lightly equipped military and civilian personnel whose task it was to reduce and control levels of violence by means other than enforcement. In contrast, under the broad and ill-defined rubric of 'peace-building', the aim of external involvements in the post-Cold War period has been couched in far more ambitious terms: to support 'political, institutional, and social transformations necessary to overcome deep-seated internal animosities and strife'.[5] The sheer level of ambition here – specifically the *transformative* commitment on the part of external actors – is striking and, in important respects, the suggestion that contemporary peacebuilding has sought to 'compress into a few years evolutions that have taken centuries' contains more than a grain of truth.[6] What has been driving this development?

Until the terrorist attacks on New York and Washington in September 2001, efforts to account for the 'new interventionism' in Western academic and policy discourse attached special significance to the decisive influence of normative developments in international relations since the end of the Cold War.[7] Indeed, the prominence given to the protection of basic human rights, the establishment of the rule of law and democracy promotion as drivers of intervention were seen by some as evidence of an ever-widening commitment to the tenets of liberal internationalism.[8] The declaratory endorsement by UN member states in September 2005 of the idea that they shared a 'responsibility to protect' populations 'from genocide, war crimes, ethnic cleansing and crimes against humanity' should national governments or authorities 'manifestly' fail in their own duty to do so has been taken by some observers as further evidence of far-reaching and dramatic normative change.[9] Others have actively championed the idea, and looked for evidence of new 'cosmopolitan' forms of peacekeeping and peacebuilding in which considerations of 'human security' have come to transcend those of state interest and power politics.[10] For all this, while the 1990s saw a dramatic increase in external involvements precipitated by humanitarian concerns – with the NATO-led operation in Kosovo in the spring of 1999 the apotheosis of this development – to explain the pattern of post-Cold War intervention in war-torn societies solely or even primarily by reference to changes in normative context was never entirely convincing. As international-relations scholar Adam Roberts cautioned in the aftermath of NATO's Kosovo campaign, the fact that 'humanitarian issues played a historically unprecedented role in international politics' in the 1990s did not mean that there had also been 'a fundamental departure from the system of sovereign states and power politics'.[11] The inevitable and often uneasy coexistence of altruistic motives with the interest-based and power-political considerations of intervening powers and coalitions of states has always been there, though it has become more acute and has been brought into much sharper relief since the events of September 2001 and the subsequent wars in Afghanistan and Iraq. Appreciating the admixture of motives that prompts outside involvement in war-shattered countries is essential to understanding both the diversity of interventions and their decidedly uneven record of achievement.[12] It is also essential to any realistic assessment of the prospects for a more systematic, coordinated and effective international response to the challenges of peace consolidation and contemporary peacebuilding.

Whatever the complexity and shifting character of motivations, however, the general trend that this book sets out to examine is unmistakable: neither the peacekeeping failures of the early and mid 1990s, in Angola, Somalia, Rwanda and Bosnia, nor the changes in the strategic environment spawned by the events of 11 September and their aftermath, have weakened a trend that has seen 'a continued increase in international peacebuilding in the face of the enormous practical and legitimacy challenges'.[13] Indeed, if anything, interest in the subject – whether it is measured in terms of new missions or of the institutional provisions increasingly made for 'post-conflict', 'peacebuilding' or 'stability' operations within the decision-making machinery of states and international organisations and among armed forces – has intensified since 2003.[14] According to the Stockholm International Peace Research Institute (SIPRI), 60 multilateral peace operations, involving a record number of nearly 190,000 military and civilian personnel, were deployed worldwide in 2008.[15] The increase in the size and number of missions with a peacebuilding mandate has been particularly pronounced on the African continent since 2003, with new deployments and existing ones significantly expanded in Côte d'Ivoire, Burundi, the DRC and Sudan. In 2007, an EU military mission, established 'in concert' with the UN, was authorised to deploy to the Central African Republic (CAR) and Chad following the abandonment of a more ambitious plan for a large-scale UN mission.[16] In Afghanistan, NATO has sought – since 2003 through its leadership of the International Security

Assistance Force (ISAF) and, in 2004 and 2005, with the establishment throughout the country of Provincial Reconstruction
Teams (PRTs) – to expand the reach and control of government
and to 'facilitate development and reconstruction'.[17] Since May
2003, a US-led international coalition has been engaged in a
violent struggle in Iraq, the declared objective of which has
been framed as the creation of 'a democratic and sovereign
nation, underpinned by new and protected freedoms and a
growing market economy'.[18]

Paralleling these developments, a large number of Western
governments have either created new bodies or reorganised
the machinery of central government concerned with
foreign, defence and development policy to better support
'post-conflict' peacebuilding activities. Such processes of institutional adaptation are ongoing in many countries.[19] As if to
underline the trend, one of the few practical outcomes of the
UN World Summit in September 2005 was the creation of the
UN Peacebuilding Commission (PBC), a move that was widely
considered to be both innovative and overdue.[20]

The full implications for governments and international
organisations of the trend towards more intrusive and ambitious post-war interventions are beyond the scope of this book.
The focus here is more restricted, though the canvas is wide.
Drawing on the experience of operations from Cambodia to
Iraq, the book is concerned with the nature of the challenges
that have confronted outside military-cum-civilian forces
engaged – with limited resources and for limited periods of
time – in 'post-conflict peacebuilding'. Such a broad and
ambitious focus necessarily demands further clarification. In
particular, it requires some discussion of the notion of 'post-
conflict peacebuilding'; a requirement that is only heightened
by the acute lack of precision with which the term has tended
to be employed in public as well as in academic and policy

discourse. Defining and clarifying the term is not, however, merely intended as a path-clearing exercise to make an amorphous and ill-defined subject area more manageable, important as that is. It also draws attention to some of the specific issues and underlying concerns that inform this book.

Definitions and scope

Definitions, it has been wisely suggested, 'are best worked towards, not stated at the outset' since 'any definition involves terms which themselves have to be defined, and so on ad infinitum – and infinite tedium'.[21] Certainly, the study of international relations is replete with terms and concepts that are necessarily contested, and discussions about their true meaning can all too easily acquire (and often have) an overly introspective and self-referential character. No doubt it is sometimes 'better to establish what one is talking about by doing the talking first'.[22] Even so, basic distinctions and working definitions do need to be established, if only to delineate more precisely one's focus of enquiry. Moreover, exploring the origins and widespread use of certain terms is usually also illuminating of wider trends and, crucially, may help to reveal unspoken assumptions that, on closer inspection, turn out to be questionable and problematic.[23] For all three of these reasons, 'post-conflict peacebuilding' – a vague and all-encompassing term around which an academic industry has grown up – merits further reflection.

The term was first introduced in 1992 in 'An Agenda for Peace', an influential though overly optimistic effort by then-UN Secretary-General Boutros Boutros-Ghali to assess the implications for the UN of the end of the Cold War. Boutros-Ghali defined the term broadly to cover 'action to identify and support structures which will tend to strengthen and solidify peace in order to avoid a relapse into conflict'.[24] The concept has remained closely associated with the UN, and is now treated as one of its core functions in the peace and security field. A survey of activities loosely subsumed under the term features annually in the Report of the Secretary-General on the Work of the Organization, and the concept has been the subject of numerous, often interminable, General Assembly and Security Council debates.[25] The UN definition of peacebuilding has remained exceedingly broad, and if anything become even broader, covering 'integrated and coordinated actions aimed at addressing the root causes of violence, whether political, legal, institutional, military, humanitarian, human rights-related, environmental, economic and social, cultural or demo-graphic'.[26] It is a definition that certainly cannot be faulted for leaving anything out. Crucial to the UN understanding of the concept is also the insistence that actions in these widely different spheres are 'mutually reinforcing'.

For an organisation long shackled by Cold War rivalry and with a membership that reflects global inequities and socio-economic disparities more accurately than any other body, the UN definition conveys a profound and laudable aspiration: to shift the focus of attention and operational activity away from simply the alleviation of violent conflict to something altogether more positive and ambitious. This is an aspiration that is also implicit in much of the peacebuilding literature, especially that which has grown out of peace and conflict studies. From both an analytical and a policymaking perspective, however, this expansive understanding of 'post-conflict peacebuilding', and the implied challenge that it poses for those undertaking it, suffers from two weaknesses.

Firstly, as former Vice-President of the International Peace Institute Elizabeth Cousens has noted, the catch-all definition used by the UN and too often uncritically recited in the literature presents the analyst and the policymaker with a 'melange of goals, conservative and ambitious, short- and long-term, that remain relatively undifferentiated, let alone considered in strategic relationship with one another'.[27] In UN documents, the statements of government ministers and the language of many non-governmental organisations, the term is virtually synonymous with the 'entire basket of post-war needs' in countries and societies emerging from violent conflict.[28] What is missing, in short, is any sense of priorities; any sense that the long list of desirable and, in their own right, entirely justifiable peacebuilding goals may not in fact be 'mutually reinforcing' in the short to medium term.

Secondly, approaches to peacebuilding – both in a UN context and in parts of the peacebuilding literature – have displayed a marked tendency to abstract the tasks of peacebuilding from their political, cultural and historical context. All too often, the result has been an ahistorical and static view of the challenges posed to outside intervention in war-torn societies and a consequent failure to take account of the variety of ways in which the past constrains, shapes and imposes limits on what outsiders can realistically achieve. This tendency has encouraged a social-engineering approach to the concept of peacebuilding. It also helps to explain why external actors have persistently failed to gauge the extent to which their own actions, policies and historical baggage necessarily contribute to shaping the 'post-conflict environment', whether through the stirring of nationalisms or through the legitimisation or delegitimisation of indigenous power structures, or by empowering or disempowering what are, for better or worse, key local actors. A particularly unfortunate aspect of this penchant for abstraction has been the recurring failure to acquire, let alone make use of, knowledge of local conditions and realities. Such knowledge, as the experience of the past two decades has shown all too clearly, is critical to a deeper understanding of the politics, society and patterns of violence characteristic of post-conflict settings. The sources of this tendency to dehistoricise and depoliticise the subject of peacebuilding are multiple and beyond the scope of this study. It is nonetheless worth noting that one effect of modern social-science methodology, specifically in its positivist, rational-choice variety, has been to reinforce the social-engineering approach that has dominated the discourse and practice of peacebuilding.[29]

This book may be viewed as an attempt to address these two weaknesses. In what way, then, does it attempt to do so? With respect to the focus of enquiry and the lack of precision highlighted by Cousens, the study draws a basic distinction – blurred in the peacebuilding literature, though admittedly hard to define in practice – between the critical phase that follows the end of major hostilities and/or the signature of a peace accord, and the longer-term challenges of rebuilding war-torn societies. While the Brahimi report on UN peace operations published in 2000 defined 'peacebuilding activities' as those 'undertaken on the far side of conflict,' the focus here is primarily on the other end of the spectrum: on the period when levels of insecurity are high; when violence is pervasive; when institutions are rudimentary, weak or non-existent; and when the very distinction between war and peace is blurred.[30] This period may, and often does, come in the immediate aftermath of violent conflict. This statement, however, requires an immediate and important qualification. The distinction between phases is not simple and clear-cut; it is broad and often hazy and, indeed, cannot be defined in purely temporal terms, with the implication this usually carries of a sequential approach to tasks to be taken by external military and civilian actors.[31] Nor should the period be understood in purely negative or risk-filled terms: it is better seen as a unique kind of political space, shaped by fatigue, uncertainty and war-weariness, but also by the hope that a new political dispensation will result in rapid improvements to quality of life.

While the distinction between phases allows for a more precise focus than that captured by the term 'post-conflict peacebuilding', this is not the sole reason for drawing it. It is also the case that the long-term outcome of an intervention – ultimately, its success or failure – may be determined during this 'first' period, as it provides the crucial opportunities for getting things right or badly wrong.[32] This book is concerned, in other words, with the nature of that period of external intervention during which the long-term outcome of the intervention may be said to hang in the balance, and with the policy challenges that are presented in this time. This is the period when the trade-offs and the difficult policy choices arise, when expectations are high but when the best may also be the enemy of the good. The trade-offs arise from the tension that exists in conflict-ridden and fractured societies emerging from war between, on the one hand, the requirements of security and political stability in the short term and, on the other, policy objectives vital to long-term stability and 'sustainable peace'. The latter range from issues related to the administration of post-conflict justice, the disarmament, demobilisation and reintegration of armed factions and combat against organised crime in zones of conflict, to the broader aims of democratisation and economic development. The former include, more narrowly, physical security, the creation and stabilisation of administrative and governance structures, and provision for the basic and life-sustaining needs of local populations, objectives all geared towards keeping peace alive or a fragile 'peace process' afloat.

The tension between short and long-term objectives is, of course, highly context-specific and the degree of incompatibility between immediate 'post-conflict' priorities and long-term peacebuilding objectives should not be overdrawn. Even in the best of circumstances, however, a perfect reconciliation of long-term objectives with the more immediate tasks of stabilisation has proved hard to achieve, and it is an underlying theme of this book that trade-offs, priority-setting and awkward compromises between these sets of objectives simply cannot be avoided, however much UN documents and government communiqués may insist on the 'mutually reinforcing' character of all peacebuilding objectives.[33] The difficulties and risks involved in making judgements about appropriate policy choices against this reality are real, made all the more so by the limited time horizons of outside actors and the fact that the resources they bring to bear – financial, human and diplomatic – are not only finite but also reflect and are continuously subject to a complex of political pressures and constraints emanating from their own domestic contexts. The cases covered here offer examples of both the obvious dangers involved: the derailment of the whole of a mission through a failure to prioritise short-term objectives aimed at stabilising the immediate post-conflict environment, and the risk of letting short-term objectives undermine, perhaps fatally, long-term prospects for stability founded on institutions and practices that command deep and genuine legitimacy.[34]

A stark example of the issues involved, which also makes the argument less abstract, is provided by the 'opium dilemma' in Afghanistan: that is, the ongoing challenge for the Afghan government and its external supporters – NATO, the UN and bilateral donors – posed by illegal opium production in war-torn and impoverished Afghanistan.[35] Interestingly, how best to meet this challenge has been a source of deep policy division between the US and its principal ally, the UK.[36] On the one hand, there is little doubt that illegal opium production in Afghanistan – accounting for over 90% of world production, increasingly tied to illicit regional and global networks of processing and trade, and an integral part of Afghanistan's war economy benefiting not only the Taliban but also government officials and international criminal networks – has become a fundamental 'obstacle to long-term security and development'.[37] At the same time, as the International Council on Security and Development (ICSD) has repeatedly warned, the 'wrong sequencing in counter-narcotics strategies can severely affect the economies and stability of rural communities and lead to higher political risks for the country as a whole'.[38] The fact is, as academic and former Afghan Interior Minister Ali Jalabi has plainly put it, 'destroying one-third of Afghanistan's economy without undermining stability requires enormous resources, administrative capacity and time'.[39] All three of these requirements are in short supply. Such warnings nonetheless imply that the unintended consequences of some policy options are less likely to be damaging than those of others, and forcible crop eradication in the absence of alternative livelihoods and rural development, a strategy that has been favoured by the US government, would seem particularly ill-advised in current circumstances.[40] Yet all the options discussed, including the licensing of opium for medical purposes as proposed by the ICSD, are fraught with problems and costs in the short and medium term.[41]

The case of illegal opium production in Afghanistan draws attention to a final consideration. Highlighting what are at times complex and morally uncomfortable policy dilemmas is not to reject the values of liberalism that have provided an important impetus for the growth of peacebuilding activity since the early 1990s, nor is it to deny their crucial role in providing the regulative ideas and the broad directions of policy. What it, and this book, does, however, is to challenge what distinguished late philosopher Leszek Kolakowski described as a 'certain innate optimism' characteristic of liberal philosophy that has also permeated liberal discourse on peacebuilding: an optimism consisting of the tendency 'to believe that there is a good solution for every situation and not that circumstances will arise in which the available solutions are not only bad, but very bad'.[42]

Argument in brief

It would be both presumptuous and impractical to seek to address the full range of issues raised by efforts to consolidate peace following violent conflict in the post-Cold War era.[43] The choice of cases and themes here – as well as the balance the book seeks to strike between breadth and depth of coverage – is intended to bring out the key issues and lessons to have emerged from the experience of the past two decades. Inevitably, the choices made reflect certain judgements and priorities on the author's part, and it is useful at this stage to reiterate what is and what is not being attempted.

The primary focus, especially in Chapters 1 and 2, is on the immediate task of consolidation and stabilisation presented to an outside force in the aftermath of armed conflict. As indicated above, this phase of operations is critical to the long-term outcome of any peacebuilding intervention. At the same time, there is an underlying recognition throughout the book that the distinction between 'war' and 'peace' – much like that between 'conflict' and 'post-conflict' – is always likely to be blurred, and that it would be futile to seek to define the length of the early and critical period with any great degree of precision. Likewise, this study and its findings – as Chapter 3, which looks at the policy and organisational responses of governments and international organisations to the challenge of peacebuilding, makes clear – recognise that the decisions taken during the early phase cannot be neatly separated from many of the longer-term challenges covered in greater depth in the burgeoning literature on state-building.

The book begins by exploring the nature and characteristics of the 'peacebuilding' environment. The range and variety of operational settings covered is vast, and an underlying theme is that simple generalisations and direct comparisons between environments are both problematic and risky. That said, international efforts to consolidate peace from Cambodia to Iraq do point to certain cross-cutting categories of issues through which the history and experience of different interventions may be approached, and it is important to scrutinise these, as each has served to shape and constrain the activities of outsiders.

Three priority tasks, all intimately connected, stand out for outside forces in the critical post-war phase in each of the diverse environments examined: the establishment of a secure environment, the stabilisation of governing structures, and provision for the uninterrupted flow of basic, life-sustaining services. Driving activities in support of these aims should be an overriding concern with the building of legitimacy, both for the intervening force itself and for the administrative and governance structures on whose proper functioning the consolidation of peace depends. Building legitimacy in turn requires a deep understanding of the contextual categories alluded to above, and the way in which these come together to shape and define the 'post-conflict' environment. It is the lack of such understanding that has too often doomed peacebuilding endeavours to ineffectiveness.

With these issues in mind, the final section of the book examines the organisational and policy responses to peacebuilding challenges. In addressing the ways in which governments and international organisations have responded to these challenges, the analysis moves beyond immediate 'post-conflict' tasks to look at the relationship of these to longer-term objectives and priorities. The UN, in particular its Peacebuilding Commission (PBC) and the associated peacebuilding 'architecture', is an important case study here, primarily because the UN is, and is likely to remain, a dominant actor in the peacebuilding field, and because the challenges that the PBC was designed to address – how to improve strategic coordination, enhance efficiency in the marshalling and delivery of resources, and increase responsiveness to local needs – raise broader issues of policy in relation to peacebuilding. These are issues that also face individual governments and other international organisations. Fashioning policy and creating organisational structures to support peacebuilding is not a mere technocratic exercise; actual outcomes are inescapably marked by bureaucratic and international politics, that is, by competition over resources, priorities and policies among bureaucracies and member states. The history and functioning of the PBC illustrate this clearly, and thus the commission serves as a microcosm of wider challenges facing international peacebuilding efforts.

Drawing lessons from 'post-conflict' interventions

The 'post-conflict' interventions of the post-Cold War era have assumed a variety of forms and their legal and moral bases have often been the subject of controversy, in many cases passionately so. This does not invalidate the attempt to compare cases and draw wider lessons from efforts to consolidate peace after hostilities. Comparisons can be highly instructive in pointing to larger issues and problems when intervening in societies ravaged by war and violent conflict. Thus, the challenges facing American forces in Iraq since the spring of 2003 – high levels and multiple sources of insecurity, the struggle to imbue the intervention with political legitimacy, the difficulties of providing local communities with essential services – are present, while obviously not to the same degree, in all post-conflict settings.[44]

Iraq provides here, as in many other instances, an extreme example of some basic and recurring challenges. Likewise, the experience of international involvement in Somalia over the past two decades, while unique in key respects, highlights the vital importance of understanding the 'local political culture' within an area of operation.[45] It may be objected that the efforts over the past ten years to stabilise and bring peace to the DRC relate to an unrepresentative case from which it is difficult to draw wider lessons. Again, however, the value of that country as a case study is precisely that it presents in heightened form aspects of the 'peacebuilding challenge' also evident in other cases: the need to understand how the political economy of an armed conflict shapes its 'post-conflict' environment, how wars mutate and acquire long-lasting regional and transnational dimensions, how the resources and political commitments of those assuming peacebuilding responsibilities help define what can and cannot realistically be achieved.

It should be evident already that the use of the term 'post-conflict' to describe the kinds of operational settings and challenges explored in this book is strictly misleading. The term appears destined to stay, however, and this is in part why no attempt has been made to replace it here. That said, a degree of terminological inexactitude is unavoidable in dealing with this subject, and historian Hugh Seton-Watson's exculpatory plea in the introduction to one of his works seems appropriate here as well. Acknowledging that the effort to make sense of his chosen subject 'undoubtedly lacks neatness', he adds that this is 'inevitable because the subject itself is not neat'.[46]

CHAPTER ONE

The Peacebuilding Environment

From Bosnia to Iraq, Cambodia to Liberia, individual post-conflict settings all possess unique characteristics and distinctive features. This important, though oft-neglected, truism should stand as a warning against the tendency for organisations, governments and analysts to approach post-conflict challenges in terms of easily transferable templates or universally valid planning assumptions. It has been suggested, for example, that the rough ride initially encountered by the UN Transitional Administration in East Timor (UNTAET), established in October 1999, was partly the result of mistaken planning assumptions borrowed from the UN Mission in Kosovo (UNMIK), which had been set up less than half a year earlier.[1] Similarly, NATO's initial planning and preparations for its mission to Afghanistan drew too heavily, officials now readily acknowledge, on the Alliance's experiences in the Balkans.[2] In other cases, notably Iraq, thinking about post-conflict challenges has been naively and wholly inappropriately informed by the lessons supposedly offered by the transition to a market economy in Russia and Eastern Europe after the fall of communism.[3]

While the dangers of template thinking and misplaced analogous reasoning are thus very real, this does not mean that there is no scope for comparing different peacebuilding environments. The approach taken here is that while direct comparisons are always problematic and potentially misleading, assessing the uneven record of post-Cold War interventions and, by extension, examining the challenges and lessons of 'post-conflict peacebuilding' in a more generic sense can usefully be aided by framing discussion and analysis around certain contextual categories or recurring sets of issues that cut across different cases. These issues in turn generate questions that are relevant to any post-conflict situation, even though the answers to the questions will differ from case to case. Four such categories or sets of issues are identified in this chapter: political context and end-state; historical setting and psychological climate; violence, insecurity and crime; and the political economy of war and peace.

These categories are, plainly, all closely connected. Thus, the high levels of insecurity and multiple sources of violence that often characterise post-conflict settings cannot be understood in isolation from the political economy of the conflict in question. Likewise, the wider political context that distinguishes a post-conflict setting will always be influenced by the historical memories and experiences of local populations and elites, especially if those experiences involve a history of foreign occupation or, more subtle in its impact, a long-standing sense of weakness and vulnerability in the face of outside pressures and interference. But while closely connected, the categories do nonetheless serve a useful analytic purpose in allowing comparisons to be made across different cases and thus for wider conclusions to be drawn.

There is a final cautionary note that needs to be made at the outset. A deeper understanding of contextual factors will not necessarily provide clear-cut answers or obvious policy implications for an external force engaged in or contemplating intervention in a peacebuilding capacity. Indeed, the opposite will often be the case. As historian Jeremy Black has remarked about the uses of his discipline, there is a critical distinction to be drawn between history as providing 'answers' and 'history as questions offered by scholars alive to the difficulties and dangers of predicting outcomes'.[4] This is also the spirit in which the attempt to better understand the peacebuilding challenge should be approached.

Political context and end-state
The underlying stability of political settlements
The challenges involved in consolidating peace in the aftermath of armed conflict are intimately connected to the nature and quality of the political settlement that brought the active or most violent phase of that conflict to an end. The term 'settlement' in this context should be understood broadly to cover both formal agreements and informal arrangements or understandings that obtain at the end of hostilities. The essential point is that all such settlements reflect certain political realities, encompassing both conditions 'on the ground' and a distinctive balance of external pressures and influences bearing on the conflict. These realities have ranged widely, from situations of great clarity in terms of political end-state and the perceived legitimacy of the new political dispensation emerging after conflict to, at the other extreme, situations of profound ambiguity and uncertainty, more akin to a lull in fighting than the beginning of lasting peace.

The UN Operation in Eastern Slavonia (UNTAES), which between 1996 and 1998 oversaw the transfer of Eastern Slavonia from Serb to Croatian government control, is often held up, especially by those involved in the operation, as a true success

story.[5] Its success, however, was owed largely to the fact that
the political end-state was never in doubt: Croatia was reas-
serting full sovereignty within an agreed period over a piece
of territory temporarily occupied by the Krajina Serbs. The
UN operations in East Timor from 1999 to 2002 were similarly
blessed with an unambiguous political end-state: full independence from Indonesia for East Timor. While both operations
saw violence and experienced real difficulties on the ground,
the wider political context meant that the role of the outside
presence in each case was always, if never straightforward,
imbued with a critical advantage. Interestingly, both operations, in spite of an auspicious political context at the outset,
also illustrate the difficulty of deciding how – that is, by what
criteria – to measure the 'success' of post-conflict interventions. The incorporation of Eastern Slavonia into Croatia was
peaceful and this, given the recent history of the region, was
undoubtedly a major achievement. The process of incorporation, however, also intensified the exodus, encouraged by local
Croatian authorities, of much of the pre-war Serbian population from the territory of Eastern Slavonia.[6] Post-independence
East Timor (now Timor Leste), while unquestionably a better
place for being free of the cruel and oppressive quasi-colonial
rule of Indonesia, has continued to be plagued by violence and
political turmoil, prompting the UN Security Council in August
2006 to authorise a new mission to the country.[7]

In contrast to these two operations, the uncertainty that
continued to surround the future status of Kosovo after NATO's
military campaign in 1999, when the Security Council resolution establishing an international presence in the province left
its status unresolved 'pending final settlement', partly explains
why the history of the UN Mission in Kosovo has been so trou-
bled in spite of the exceptional powers and resources given to
it.[8] In Iraq and Afghanistan, the question of political end-state

appeared, to some at any rate, to have been settled by, respectively, the removal of Saddam Hussein in 2003 and the routing of the Taliban regime in 2001. In reality, of course, the absence of a clear political end-state has provided a critical backdrop to developments in both theatres ever since, as reflected in the extreme difficulty faced by incumbent regimes and their external sponsors in establishing their legitimacy throughout the territory and across sectarian and ethnic divides.

In Kosovo, the potentially destabilising effects of political uncertainty after 1999 were offset by the determination on the part of NATO and the EU – expressed in military, economic and diplomatic terms – to avoid a resurgence of large-scale violence. Even then, the challenge facing well-equipped, properly resourced and numerically superior forces was at times more than they could handle, as the riots in Mitrovica in March 2004 plainly showed.[9] Elsewhere, however, the underlying instability of political settlements – compounded by a level of international commitment nowhere near that exhibited in Kosovo after in 1999 or in Bosnia-Herzegovina following the Dayton Peace Accord in late 1995 – has enormously complicated the tasks facing 'peacebuilders' on the ground, forcing them to rely heavily on the capricious 'good faith' of the parties involved.

In November 1994, the Angolan government and rebel movement the National Union for the Total Independence of Angola (UNITA) signed the Lusaka Protocol, bringing to a temporary end the murderous civil war that had resumed after the country's first national elections in September 1992. Over the next four years, the international community – having learnt from the earlier mistake of deploying only a skeletal force to observe the 1992 elections – deployed two peacekeeping operations to the country and spent an estimated $1.5 billion on the so-called 'Lusaka Peace Process'.[10] In December 1998 that process collapsed into all-out war. While the usual problems for which UN operations and international peacebuilding efforts are often justly criticised were undoubtedly present – among them a lack of donor coordination and a slow pace of deployment of UN peacekeepers – the fundamental problem lay elsewhere. UNITA had signed up to 'peace' only when the movement had been seriously weakened by major territorial losses in 1993 and 1994, specifically the capture of the diamond fields of Saurimo and Cafunfo from which much of its funding came. The ensuing Lusaka Process, it is now clear, gave UNITA the time it needed to rearm and fight another day. The war came to an end with the death in battle of UNITA's leader Jonas Savimbi in February 2002, a man whose 'messianic sense of destiny'[11] and determination to one day rule the whole of Angola had until then precluded compromise. The speed with which the cease-fire was concluded and the progress made in consolidating peace since then, including a logistically fraught but nonetheless rapid demobilisation and reintegration of UNITA soldiers, point to the critical importance of the change in political context brought about by the death of Savimbi and, with it, the effective defeat of UNITA.[12] The transformation that followed Savimbi's death has been striking. As long-time observers of the Angolan scene Alex Vines and Bereni Oruitemeka have written: 'from being one of the most protracted conflicts in Africa, Angola became, within five years, one of the most successful economies in sub-Saharan Africa'.[13]

In other cases, the fragility of the political settlement intended to provide the basis for 'post-conflict peacebuilding' and the unsatisfactory compromises made along the way have been even more obvious than they were in 1990s Angola. Of the process that led up to the 'all-inclusive Peace Agreement' that marked the official end of the Second Congo War in December 2002, distinguished Africa scholar Gérard Prunier says: 'the whole exercise, necessary as it was to stop major organised violence, reeked of rewards for crime coupled with pork-barrel politics'.[14] Another, arguably more striking, example is provided by the peace accord and associated power-sharing deal reached, following heavy international pressure, by the government of Sierra Leone under President Tejan Kabbah and rebel group the Revolutionary United Front (RUF) led by Foday Sankoh in Lomé in Togo in July 1999. Reached six months after a murderous assault by the RUF and soldiers of the Armed Forces Revolutionary Council (AFRC) on the Sierra Leonean capital of Freetown, in which an estimated 5,000 people were killed and atrocities were widespread, the Lomé agreement not only offered Sankoh immunity from prosecution but also made him chairman of the Commission for the Management of Strategic Resources, which was 'charged with the responsibility of securing and monitoring the legitimate exploitation of Sierra Leone's gold and diamonds'.[15] As with the Abuja Accord of 1995, which had resulted in a temporary stop to the civil war in Liberia, the Lomé agreement was 'basically an effort to appease local warlords by giving them political power in exchange for military peace. Both were an open invitation for warlords to enjoy the spoils of office in a giant jumble sale of the national wares.'[16] Against this reality it was hardly surprising that the accord fell apart as quickly as it did, with the RUF/AFRC soon again 'marching towards Freetown'.[17]

It is clear, then, that the political context at the outset of post-Cold War peacebuilding operations – from the certainties underpinning the UNTAES mission in Eastern Slavonia to the extreme fragility of and deeply fraught assumptions underlying the Lomé Accord – has varied greatly. Although 'political realities' have clearly proved more auspicious in some cases than others, making judgements about the fundamental viability of a settlement, including the good faith of parties involved, is often difficult, not least because the 'realities' are not permanently fixed but can be affected by both internal and external pressures and developments. Whether or not the Lusaka Process of 1994–98 in Angola was doomed to failure is still a contested issue. Even so, the record does seem to indicate that, as a general rule, the greater the political uncertainty, the more critical is the level and quality of international commitment to nurture and support the process of consolidating peace in its early phases. The comparatively low levels of post-conflict violence in Bosnia following the war of 1992–95 owe much to the sheer scale of military, economic and diplomatic resources committed to the country by the international community after 1995.[18] That level of commitment has not been, nor is it likely to be, replicated elsewhere. It has also generated its own problems, encouraging a 'tendency towards political irresponsibility among Bosnia's domestic leaders'[19] and acting as a kind of structural disincentive against meeting long-term post-conflict challenges, especially in the economic sphere.[20] Nonetheless, the sheer weight of resources, as the case of Kosovo also makes clear, has often proved an important element in shepherding a mission through the early and most delicate phase of an operation; a time when size of the 'footprint' is also often of great psychological significance.

This discussion does, however, raise a further, more thought-provoking consideration. Writing in 1999, political scientist Edward Luttwak proposed, albeit mischievously, that a way out of the dilemma presented by the uncertainty surrounding the political end-state was to 'give war a chance'.[21] The case of Angola would appear to support his case. It was the military defeat of UNITA that in the end set the stage for the longest phase of comparative peace in Angola's history. Not only that, but victory was achieved only after 'the government embarked upon a brutal scorched earth policy... forcibly [removing] people to provincial capitals'.[22] Even so, the fundamental problem with 'giving war a chance' remains: people may be prepared to fight, at a terrible cost, for a long time, especially in civil-war situations that have acquired a zero-sum character for the participants involved. This is one reason – and it is a very good one – why governments have, on the whole, been increasingly unprepared to contemplate Luttwak's option, especially when inaction carries with it the risk of large-scale population displacement and massive violations of human rights.[23] Indeed, in the post-Cold War period it has often been the very prospect of such violations, or the readiness to deal with their consequences and prevent their recurrence, that has prompted outside intervention in the first place. International pressure, however misguided, on the parties to sign up to the Lomé Accord was partly designed to prevent slaughter on the scale witnessed six months earlier. Yet the Lomé Accord, widely seen even at the time of its signature as deeply flawed, was also a product of other factors: an unwillingness on the part of Nigeria to continue to carry the major burden of peacekeeping in Sierra Leone; the unwillingness of Western countries to assume greater responsibility for stabilising conditions on the ground (Lomé negotiations coincided with the final stages of NATO's Kosovo campaign) and, finally, an ill-judged and ill-informed role played by external mediators, specifically US President Bill Clinton's special envoy to Africa, the Reverend Jesse Jackson.[24] The larger point here is that the 'humanitarian impulse', the desire to 'demonstrate resolve' or even the well-intentioned effort to address charges of selectivity has rarely been matched by the kinds of commitments – diplomatic as well as in terms of material resources – merited by the case in question. To expect that it would in every case is plainly unrealistic and, as observed above, the case of Bosnia simply will not be replicated elsewhere. Still, the gap between 'ends' and 'means' has often been alarmingly wide. This is especially true of those operations in Africa that have grown out of what were initially more limited peacekeeping endeavours. The result in many cases has been that peace operations and peacebuilding missions have found themselves saddled with mandates that reflect awkward political compromises and conflicting pressures, thus enormously complicating the translation, by peacebuilders on the ground, of declaratory commitments into realisable goals. Indeed, this conundrum has been at the heart of the difficulties, discussed more fully in the next chapter, faced by what in 2009 is the largest and most ambitious of all UN operations: the efforts of some 16,000 peacekeepers to consolidate peace in the DRC.

Regional context: major powers and neighbouring states

The political realities that help define a peacebuilding environment are not simply the products of the internal state of play among former belligerents or the quality of the political settlement, whether implicit or explicit, they have been able to reach. As all of the cases above make clear, two additional factors play a key role.

The first is the wider regional context within which any given conflict is necessarily situated. That context includes the specific interests of neighbouring states and regional powers in relation to the conflict itself. These have often been shaped by 'special relations' and historic ties – sometimes cemented by bonds of kinship, culture and economic links that cut across official borders – between states (or influential groups within those states) and direct parties to the conflict. The regional context also includes what are best described as the wider patterns of enmity and cooperation that have historically helped to shape and define a given region or neighbourhood. Both contextual elements ensure that the intrusion of an external presence, including a seemingly benign peacebuilding operation, is never 'neutral' in its consequences, bound as it is to affect the calculations and policies not only of warring parties but also of neighbouring states and regional powers. The dynamics of internal conflicts subject to outside intervention in the post-Cold War period – in the Balkans, West Africa, Central Africa, Asia and the Middle East – simply cannot be understood without taking account of this regional dimension. Thus, the attitudes of Vietnam and Thailand towards not only the UN Transitional Authority in Cambodia (UNTAC) in 1992–93, but also towards Cambodian factions and remnants of the Khmer Rouge after the formal withdrawal of UN troops, were essential to efforts to consolidate peace. Writing on the eve of the invasion of Iraq, Charles Tripp, a leading authority on the history and politics of Iraq, warned that the US 'should regard any attempt to reconstruct the Iraqi state as an undertaking with powerful regional dimensions', noting that neighbouring states – Turkey, Iraq and Syria – all had a 'depth of intimate knowledge of aspects at least of Iraqi political society which it is very unlikely the US or its Western allies can match'.[25]

There is a further, related aspect to the regional context: the political economy of contemporary armed conflicts tends to be deeply embedded in more informal regional networks of a social, military and economic kind.[26] Such links between peoples and groups across formal frontiers – making use of long-standing, historically rooted trading and commercial networks and bene-fiting from the lack of effective state control – are important to an understanding of the dynamics of conflict and therefore also to any peacebuilding effort that follows it.[27] This is most obviously the case, as scholars Michael Pugh, Neil Cooper and Jonathan Goodhand have shown, in relation to so-called 'marginalized borderlands'; areas that often constitute 'a pivotal locus in the emergence of violent political economies and [therefore] vital area[s] in which to focus attempts to construct a post-conflict peace'.[28] Prominent examples of such borderlands include the border regions of Afghanistan and Pakistan; the Fergana Valley that straddles Tajikistan, Uzbekistan and Kyrgyzstan; the Presevo valley in southern Serbia and the territory along the Kosovo–Macedonian border; and the Kivu region in the DRC bordering Rwanda, Burundi and Uganda.

Secondly, the interests of major powers regarding a conflict will, for better or worse, influence all peacebuilding efforts in relation to it. This is true in the obvious sense that resources and commitments will tend to flow more readily to operations in which major powers perceive their interests to be at stake. This explains in part the enormous variation in commitment to different geographical regions and zones of conflict and the selectivity of engagement in the post-Cold War period. Just as important, when major powers are able to agree on a political end-state and support a peacebuilding mission through diplomatic efforts and 'positive regional engagement',[29] the scope for effective action is plainly much greater. In the post-Cold War history of UN operations the clearest examples of this are provided by UNTAC in Cambodia and the UN Operation in Mozambique (ONUMOZ), two operations with 'peacebuilding' elements to their mandates. Both operations required improvisation and creative interpretation of the original mandate by local heads of mission and force commanders, and neither operation was problem-free. In both cases, however, Security Council support remained strong and did not fracture at critical moments. In the end, this proved a key factor in the missions' success.[30] The alternative to the kind of unity and commonality of purpose displayed in regard to these missions is divisions and tensions among major powers, leading, at worst, to the competitive engagement of great powers in a zone of conflict. Even in the absence of open competition, discord among major powers can lead to agreement around only a limited set of objectives, leaving a mission without strategic direction or purpose.

Historical and psychological context

For an outside force to operate with any likelihood of success in a post-conflict society, sensitivity to the historical and cultural setting and reflexes of that society is essential. To many this will appear obvious and as hardly meriting separate treatment. Yet it is striking just how absent, beyond the superficial and glib acknowledgement that 'history matters', the significance of complex historical legacies has been from the deliberations of Western governments contemplating interventions in societies which, while fractured and traumatised by war, retain a profound sense of their own history and cultural worth, and whose basis of social order often differs sharply from those of the intervening powers. There are two closely related tendencies here that merit attention. The first is a particular and recurring blind spot of Western decision-makers: the tendency to underestimate the effects that intervention and a protracted foreign presence, however well intentioned, are likely to have in stimulating nationalist sentiments, encouraging various forms of local resistance and, more generally, in shaping the complex psychological environment of post-conflict societies. The second, alluded to in the Introduction, has been the tendency to divorce contemporary events and 'peacebuilding' challenges from their specific historical and cultural contexts, thus enormously complicating any attempts to grasp the complexities of local politics and society.

Nationalism, resistance and the psychology of post-conflict societies

The failure to gauge the effects of intervention on foreign soil is now frequently brought up in relation to the war in Iraq and its aftermath, where, it is true, the US-led invasion of 2003, whatever the mixture of motives that underlay it, powerfully stirred an Iraqi nationalism that has fuelled the subsequent 'insurgency' and resistance to occupation.[31] Having observed the occupation at close quarters during a period with the Coalition Provisional Authority in Baghdad, Larry Diamond, a social scientist with a long-standing interest in the challenges of democratisation, wrote in 2005 that:

> although most Iraqis were grateful for having been liberated from a brutal tyranny, their gratitude was mixed with deep suspicion of the US's real motives; … humiliation that the Iraqis themselves had proved unable to overthrow Saddam; and unrealistic expectations of the post-war administration … Too many Iraqis viewed the invasion not as an international effort but as an occupation by Western, Christian, essentially Anglo-American powers, and this evoked powerful memories of previous subjugation and of the nationalist struggles against Iraq's former overlords.[32]

The view that 'Iraqi patriotism' and 'revulsion at the invasion of the country by foreign armies' alone gave rise to the insurgency is of course much too crude and must be qualified, most obviously, in relation to the different historical experiences of the Kurdish, Shia and Sunni communities in the country.[33] This, however, does not invalidate the importance of the past to the understanding of contemporary events; it merely adds a layer of complexity by pointing to the differential impact of historical experiences – be it under pre-colonial, colonial or post-colonial rule – on different communities.[34] In the case of Iraq, this raises a further issue. The inability to gauge the impact of foreign intervention on Iraqi soil was compounded by an unwillingness to engage with Iraqi society on its own terms. Scholar Charles Tripp, recalling a meeting of academics arranged for the benefit of Prime Minister Tony Blair in November 2002, notes – damningly – how the prime minister 'seemed wholly uninterested in Iraq as a complex and puzzling political society'.[35] The wealth of memoir literature and insider accounts that now also exists on the US preparations for and conduct of operations after the fall of Saddam Hussein reveals a similar lack of interest in Iraq itself among key actors charged with planning post-war operations.[36] Indeed, for those civilian personnel around Donald Rumsfeld at the Pentagon most closely involved in 'post-liberation' arrangements, notably Paul Wolfowitz and Douglas Feith at the Office of Special Plans, ignorance of Iraqi society was a virtue, in that it allowed them to treat the country 'as a blank slate, to be remade in the image of its liberators'.[37] The problem, as Ali Allawi has observed with barely concealed contempt, was not just the dearth of 'systematic analysis': 'it was more a deliberate revelling in the debunking of whatever knowledge on Iraq existed'.[38] In these circumstances it was hardly surprising that the US failed to recognise how 'the invasion of Iraq would open up great fissures in Iraqi society, with enormous regional and international consequences'.[39]

As in the case of Iraq, explaining what has been dubbed the 'neo-Taliban insurgency'[40] in Afghanistan entirely in terms of a broad-based and spontaneous nationalist resistance to foreign invasion would be too simple. And yet, NATO's deepening difficulties since its assumption of full control of ISAF in 2003 cannot be understood without reference to Afghanistan's long history of resistance to foreign domination and intrusion. Indeed, according to academic commentator Anatol Lieven, given the 'history of Pashtun resistance to outside military conquest over the past 150 years, it would ... be nothing short of astonishing if a massive insurgency had not occurred'.[41] The wider point at issue here is not whether the nationalism provoked by outside intrusion is constructed or appeals to a fictitious and mythical past, nor is the suggestion here that nationalism is a simple unitary phenomenon. The key question as far as the post-conflict environment is concerned is whether those with a vested interest in continued violence succeed in appropriating and harnessing the symbols and power of nationalism to serve their own purposes. Their ability to do so depends crucially, for better or worse, on the actions of outsiders. In Afghanistan in 2005 and 2006, for example, when NATO officials increasingly discussed success and progress in language that spoke of 'body counts', 'breaking the back of the resistance' and inflicting 'decisive blows on the enemy', they were playing into the hands of the Taliban, who were easily able to make use of this kind of language in their appeal to a 'heroic' history of resistance against foreign incursion, most recently against the Soviet Union in the 1980s.

The occupation of Iraq involved, in the words of historian Corelli Barnett, 'the forcible intrusion of Western power and culture into an Arab Islamic country with its own proud cultural and religious history'.[42] When to this reality is added the well-documented failures to plan for the post-invasion phase and the bitter controversies surrounding the deeper motives for invasion, it is tempting to dismiss the case of Iraq as too atypical for wider lessons to be drawn; that is, to treat it as a special case of little relevance to an understanding of how more benign or consent-based post-conflict interventions have often stimulated local nationalisms and various degrees of resistance to a foreign presence.

This would be rash, however. The past plays powerfully into the psychological climate that characterises any post-conflict setting, whether that past involves subjugation, conflict and glory or, as is often the case, a combination of all three. Larry Diamond's observation about Iraq cited above usefully outlines some of the important themes that have frequently informed perceptions and coloured local senti-ments about incomers: suspicion of the motives of outside forces; a sense of humiliation; and heightened expectations about what peace will bring. Before the invasion of Iraq in 2003, Isam al-Khafaji, an Iraqi social scientist who served briefly on the Iraqi Reconstruction and Development Council before resigning in July 2003, remarked that 'a volatile mixture of euphoria, anxiety about the future, attempts to redress the grave injustices of more than three decades of tyranny ... would almost certainly be the order of the day once people firmly believed that Saddam's days were numbered'.[43] Such volatility, which is not unique to the Iraqi situation, is inten-sified by the sense of humiliation and vulnerability felt by many local populations in conflict situations. This sense of vulnerability, informed by historical experience and exist-ing in combination with unrealistic expectations about an immediate peace dividend, is a recurring feature of post-conflict settings, and it makes for a psychological climate that is not only volatile but which often evolves rapidly in the early phase of a post-conflict operation. It helps to explain the curious blend of elation and fear, of hope mingled with deep uncertainty about the future, that were aspects of the psychological climate in Cambodia during UNTAC's mission in 1992–93, in Kosovo in April and May 1999 and, indeed, in Iraq in the spring of 2003. Crucially, as these and other cases have shown, when expectations are not satisfied – as they can never fully be – anger and frustration often translate into increased violence and instability. Even in those cases where local support for the initial intervention and the early peace-building activities is overwhelming, indigenous reactions and responses to foreign intervention are often complex and ambivalent beneath the surface, especially when interventions turn out to be protracted and fail to deliver on public pronouncements. One example is East Timor; although outside involvement in 1999 was critical to securing independence and freedom after 25 years of Indonesian rule, it was not long before the East Timorese began to view the UN presence as a 'second occupation'.[44] The experience of this and numerous other operations shows that the presence of foreigners, 'even when they hail from liberal democratic states, and even when their stated goals [involve] protecting society and making it more secure', has the effect of 'shift[ing] the psychological balance' in a post-conflict setting.[45]

How should the particular blind spot with regard to the power of nationalism be explained? Insofar as one is dealing with interventions conceived by liberal democracies and driven by liberal ideals, the neglect may be seen as another manifestation of the tendency, noted by Isaiah Berlin, for 'rationalists and liberals' to 'virtually ignore nationalism', dismissing it as 'a mere sign of immaturity, an irrational relic of, or retrogressive return to, a barbarous past'.[46] Certainly, a belief in the rightness of the cause – to wit, promoting democracy, defending human rights and instilling liberal values – appears to discourage reflection on the possibility that local reactions to foreign intrusion may be conditioned by complex historical legacies. In many of the places where Western powers have intervened, the strongest such legacy is often that of colonial history in all its phases: conquest; rule and 'pacification' and, above all, the often bloody process of decolonisation. As historians Christopher Bayly and Tim Harper have observed, 'the darker underside' of this history 'has rarely been told'; this, perhaps, is also why decision-makers have often neglected its ongoing relevance to contemporary perceptions.[47]

The impact and variety of historical settings

Anthropologists and historians concerned with the richness and diversity of the societies and regions where the international community has assumed peacebuilding responsibilities after the Cold War have also drawn attention to more subtle ways in which history casts long shadows over contemporary developments and, especially, to how these may help to explain enduring patterns and forms of violence.

One comparatively well-researched case is that of Somalia, a country where, since the debacle in the streets and alleyways of Mogadishu in 1993, more than a dozen internationally sponsored peace and mediation attempts have manifestly failed to deliver stability in the south of the country. As scholar and authority on the Horn of Africa Ken Menkhaus has shown, the reason stems largely from a failure to tailor peacebuilding initiatives to the historical and cultural specificities of Somali society; specificities that include a deep suspicion of central government, an innate sense of superiority shared by all Somalis, and the vital and continuing importance of clan and kinship affiliations to the workings of Somali politics.[48] Similarly, the civil wars that erupted in West Africa in the 1990s and the attempts to restore peace in their aftermath cannot be divorced from the 'longue durée of West African history', including the precolonial history of relations between coast-based elites and the peoples of the interior.[49] Among the range of 'historical factors' that help explain modern Sudan's almost continuous history of civil wars are 'patterns of governance' inherited from Sudanic states before the nineteenth century and a 'particular brand of militant Islam' introduced in that century.[50] And of modern Afghan history, it has been said that 'any government or official political movement ...whatever its proclaimed goals and position on the left–right continuum, recruited mobilized support and operated according to criteria of ethnic/tribal/clan solidarity', and that 'political conflicts ... have stemmed from the attempts of dominant communally based elites to accomplish a high degree of centralization of power with help of foreign patrons'.[51] The contemporary relevance of these realities is plainly evident in the record of outside efforts to bring stability to Afghanistan since 2001, just as the dynamics and recurring patterns of violence in Somalia, West Africa and Sudan cannot be abstracted from their historical contexts. As an assessment of conflict in the Horn of Africa that resonates with other regions has shown: 'outsiders need to take account of the long history of amity and enmity in the region as a whole, recognising that protagonists in contemporary conflicts experience them as part of a long continuum of warfare'.[52]

As these examples suggest, the failure to place contemporary conflict in proper historical context is particularly striking in relation to Africa, a disturbing fact given the preponderance of post-conflict interventions on the continent. Indeed, some Africanists have despairingly, if justifiably, suggested that 'it seems to be the enduring fate of Africa to be "explained" in terms which are so ahistorical as to be risible'.[53] In a similar vein, Dominique Jacquin-Berdal has persuasively shown how misleading and deeply unhelpful can be the notion of 'new wars' and the writings the concept has prompted to attempts to understand contemporary patterns of violence and conflict in Africa.[54]

Precisely because historical experience and the meaning with which is it imbued by different societies is so varied it is difficult to draw simple conclusions under this heading. All these examples nonetheless reinforce James Mayall's more general observation: the past 'will continue to constrain and shape developments' in the present and for this reason there will always be 'a limit to what can be done by social engineering'.[55] The generalised character of this conclusion does not make it any less profound or pertinent, and it further highlights the need for outsiders contemplating involvement or engaging in peacebuilding also to engage with societies on their own terms.

Violence, crime and insecurity

Societies subject to intervention and post-conflict peacebuilding since the early 1990s have typically witnessed high levels of violence after the formal end of armed conflict. Violence in this context means the deliberate infliction of physical harm on people and/or damage to objects and property whether public, communal or individual.[56] Iraq in the years following the 2003 invasion offers a particularly striking example of a 'post-war' environment scarred by continuing and widespread violence. El Salvador and Guatemala – both routinely presented as success stories in the peacebuilding literature – have also seen exceptional levels of social and political violence since the end of civil war in 1992 and 1996 respectively.[57] In both these cases, overall levels of violence have remained very high.[58] Indeed, in Guatemala, data collected ten years on from the peace agreement pointed to a 'peacetime' rate of extra-judicial killings higher than at any time during the war.[59] Both countries also experienced a veritable 'crime wave' in the immediate aftermath of the signing of the peace accords, with El Salvador witnessing, according to UN figures, a 300% increase in crime in the period from January to September 1993 alone.[60] Mozambique and Liberia also experienced soaring levels of violent crime, especially in and around their respective capitals of Maputo and Monrovia, in the early years following the conclusion of peace accords in 1992 and 2003.[61] Haiti, on whose territory the UN has deployed five peacebuilding missions since the departure of the military junta led by Raoul Cédras in late 1994, has been similarly plagued by endemic and growing levels of violence. By late 2006, organised crime, revolving around illicit trafficking in 'drugs, arms and contraband', had infested and corrupted state institutions in Haiti to such a degree that a complete collapse of the state appeared imminent.[62]

Iraq, El Salvador, Guatemala and Haiti represent extreme cases in terms of the level and intensity of post-war violence. In contrast, Sierra Leone, the scene of a brutal decade-long civil war, has overall experienced comparatively low levels of violence, both in absolute and relative terms, since the end of the war in 2001.[63] Even so, stability is fragile and violence seemingly never far from the surface, with the country witnessing in March 2009 an 'outbreak of political violence and intolerance' whose emergence in the context of the country's recent relative peacefulness was 'sudden and worrying'.[64] Moreover, Sierra Leone's comparative calm makes it an exception, though significant and noteworthy for that very reason. In cases where the long-term trend has been fairly positive (i.e., showing a marked decline in the intensity of violence over time), violence has still been a distinguishing feature of the post-conflict landscape, especially in the immediate aftermath of war. In Bosnia, where levels of violence were low compared to many other post-war settings, 'murders, arson attacks, and riots against minorities who attempted to return' were still 'daily events' in the early post-Dayton years.[65] In Cambodia, government forces and troops loyal to royalist party FUNCINPEC continued to fight remnants of the Khmer Rouge until early 1999, that is, eight years after the signing of the Paris Peace Agreements.[66] In short, all of the societies covered in this book have suffered, to varying degrees, from the phenomenon of 'residual violence'[67] in the post-conflict phase.

Such violence invariably breeds fear and a deep sense of insecurity about the future. It undermines faith in governing structures and encourages the search for alternative solutions, including exile (especially among middle and professional classes), organised crime, vigilantism and other forms of 'self-policing' and 'popular justice'. In many cases, a vicious circle is thus set in motion, as crime and vigilantism themselves become major sources of violence and insecurity. Confronting post-conflict violence is therefore a central challenge facing any peacebuilding endeavour.

While the observation that post-conflict societies are often deeply violent is not itself new, much less attention has been given by policymakers and peacebuilders to the possible logic and functions of violence in such societies. Indeed, the short-hand description of post-conflict environments as 'anarchic', 'collapsed' or 'chaotic' reveals an undifferentiated approach to the central problem of violence. Related to and contributing to this, the portrayal of contemporary civil wars has suffered from a neglect of what have been aptly termed 'the micro-foundations of war', that is, the role of 'local – village, town, community – and personal dynamics' in the generation and perpetuation of violence.[68] Summarising recent research that has sought to rectify the imbalance between macro- and micro-perspectives on violence in civil wars, Susan Woodward has stressed the importance of also looking 'to fundamentally personal and local (as opposed to national) causes, not to the causal narrative of macropolitics'.[69]

All of this is of much more than academic interest since the task of providing security necessarily requires an under-standing of the varieties and sources of violence that coexist in post-conflict settings. Such an understanding demands not only an appreciation of the historical context, socio-cultural back-drop and local roots and dynamics of violence, but also of how different forms of violence overlap, interact and, inevitably in any post-war setting, tend to merge and become increasingly difficult to separate on the ground.[70] Nowhere, perhaps, has this been more evident than in the case of Iraq after the 2003 invasion, when, in the words of Phil Williams, the country became 'a "perfect storm" of organised crime and corruption', with criminal activities having 'become the funding mechanism of choice, as well as a means to consolidate control, for most of the actors engaged in violence in Iraq'.[71] This blurring of agendas is far from unique to post-Cold War conflicts. In their account of the turmoil and 'forgotten wars' that engulfed much of the 'great crescent' from Bengal to Singapore following the defeat of Japan in the Second World War, Bayly and Harper observe of the situation in Malaya in 1945 that 'the distinction between patriotism and criminality was merely one of perspective'.[72] That observation captures the reality of many contemporary peacebuilding settings, with the history and evolution of the Kosovo Liberation Army only one, albeit a particularly striking, example. In the Po Valley in Italy, the end of the Second World War was followed by a 'formidable crime wave' that involved 'hundreds of summary executions, as well as thousands of assaults, lynchings, abductions, robberies and beatings'.[73] This wave of violence, which lasted for three years within the so-called 'Triangle of Death', was 'motivated in part by pure revenge, but also by a desire to clear the ground for wider social and political revolution'.[74]

While these reflections draw attention to the complexity and multifaceted nature of post-conflict violence as a phenomenon, they also underscore the central importance of trying to distinguish analytically between categories and motivations. High levels of post-war violence are not inevitable, and the record of peacebuilding since the early 1990s makes it clear that the actions of outsiders have played a role, for better or worse, in influencing both the levels and the character of such violence. In assessing that record and for the purpose of analysis, it is helpful to distinguish between three broad – though clearly overlapping – categories of post-conflict violence. The first of these is the persistence into the post-conflict phase of political violence. The second is criminal violence, though as a conceptual category this requires a further distinction to be made between opportunistic criminal behaviour and more organised activities. Finally, there are what may be described as 'historically and culturally embedded' forms of violence.

'War after the war': political violence in post-conflict settings

The formal end of armed conflict rarely entails a clean break from past patterns of violence. This is especially the case in situations where civil or intra-state wars have been brought to an end through a negotiated settlement. Even in cases where one side has been victorious on the battlefield, political violence often continues into the post-war phase. The reason for this is, at one level, simple. While fighting and large-scale violence may die down with the official end of hostilities, the issues and grievances that first gave rise to armed conflict are unlikely to have been comprehensively addressed to the satisfaction of the many parties involved. In these circumstances, one should not expect the ideas, convictions and underlying value systems that inspired men and women to take up arms simply to have ceased to exert their influence on the outlook and positions of former enemies. This holds true whether those ideas originated in a perceived need to challenge or to defend a given social, political and economic order. It also holds true whether the ideas resonate with the liberal conscience, or whether they are found shocking and unacceptable to it. Irrespectively, they continue to influence the actions and behaviour of parties within a post-conflict environment. Given this reality, politically inspired violence – violence aimed at advancing political ends and objectives – is always likely to survive into the post-war period, even though it will inevitably coexist and merge with other sources and forms of violence.

As noted earlier, several of the peace accords that were designed to bring internal armed conflicts to an end in the 1990s – including the Bicesse Accords in Angola in 1991, the Arusha Accord concluded between the government of Rwanda and the Rwandan Patriotic Front in August 1993, the Paris Peace Agreements for Cambodia, and the peace accords for El Salvador and Guatemala – while presented to the outside world as 'comprehensive settlements', were, in reality, little of the sort. The case of the peace accord for El Salvador that was reached in Chapultepec in Mexico in early 1992, which officially brought to an end a civil war that should be understood against the backdrop of 'a long historical process of economic marginality, social segregation, and political repression', is a good example of a peace agreement that skirted, or at best dealt only incompletely with, key issues at the heart of the conflict, most notably the highly unequal concentration of land and economic power.[75] As Alvaro de Soto and Graciana del Castillo, two former UN officials who had been involved in securing a successful negotiated settlement to the El Salvador conflict, recognise: 'the problem of land was as much a root cause of the armed conflict that raged throughout the 1980s as was the overbearing power of the armed forces'.[76] Yet they also accept that, notwithstanding the success of the peace process, the peace agreement was 'not an attempt at land reform or a mechanism for income distribution'.[77] In this sense, Mo Hume, an academic who has examined post-war violence in El Salvador, is right to stress that too sharp a distinction between wartime and 'post-war' violence does not 'capture important historic and political continuities in both the dynamic of war and the structural bases of violence'.[78]

Under such circumstances of unfinished civil wars, post-conflict violence may assume not only the predictable form of score-settling and revenge killings but also continued attempts at political annihilation of opponents, either as part of an ongoing 'war after the war' or as a more deliberate regrouping of forces in anticipation of renewed war. Just as during the war itself, the aim may be to establish 'realities' on the ground more favourable to those perpetrating the violence. Politically driven violence of this sort is often aimed at 'targeted groups', that is, 'groups singled out for victimisation based on some definable characteristic' such as membership of or perceived association with a political, religious and/or sectarian group.[79] Michael Boyle, a social scientist who has studied post-war violence in a number of different contexts, describes this as 'strategic violence after wars'; 'politically instrumental violence' whose fundamental aim is to alter 'the balance of power and resources within a contested area' and which is, as such, conceptually distinct from expressive or retributive forms of violence.[80] Strategic violence of this sort assumes different forms and Boyle usefully distinguishes between four types, all of which have featured in post-conflict settings: targeted killings and assassinations aimed at 'prominent individuals or state offi-cials'; 'riots and pogroms, in which local elites and angry mobs conspire to kill or expel parts of a ... population'; 'symbolic attacks' on, for example, religious sites; and, finally, reprisals.[81] Boyle further points out that 'revenge' attacks often provide 'cover' for strategic or politically instrumental violence aimed, for example, at clearing 'territory of unwanted groups, [chang-ing] electoral fortunes within a contested area or [claiming] important economic resources'.[82]

Prominent among those instigating, sponsoring and perpe-trating this kind of violence are, unsurprisingly, those who stand to lose most from any new political dispensation. Chief among these – and of particular importance to the early chal-lenge of post-conflict stabilisation – are members of the security services and their political patrons, who will have acquired privileges under the 'old regime' and in the course of war.

According to Toby Dodge, writing in 2005, remnants of the Ba'ath Party security services were responsible for as much as 60% of the politically motivated violence in Iraq.[83] In 1992 and 1993, the period immediately following the peace accord in El Salvador was marked by a number of political assassinations of leaders and supporters of the FMLN (the guerrilla organisation that became a legal political party with the signing of the peace accord) perpetrated by 'clandestine' groups linked to the security services.[84] Similar groups were also active in Guatemala following the signing of the peace accord there in late 1996.[85] Among the targets of this violence have been members of the same political categories and constituencies as were targeted during the civil war: political leaders, priests, judges and journalists.[86] Political leaders and journalists have also been prominent victims of political violence in Lebanon since the signing of the Taif agreement that brought the civil war to a formal end in 1989, with one detailed study covering the period between 1989 and 2007 reaching the conclusion that 'political violence was both more frequent and more widespread than is often assumed'.[87] Indeed, using successful and attempted political assassinations as a measure of political violence, the study emphasised the 'remarkable continuity in the killing of political opponents from the 1950s up to the present', and concluded that 'killing political opponents is not an aberration but better understood as a political discourse carrying political messages'.[88]

There is of course nothing new about this; history affords numerous examples of politically driven violence, arising both out of wars themselves and out of the issues over which they were fought, continuing to shape post-war and post-revolutionary settings. Historian David Andress, in his reappraisal of the Terror during the French Revolution – an extended period of bloodletting that has inspired much reflection on the nature and functions of revolutionary violence – has stressed the degree to which the Terror was 'a civil war, deriving its grim impetus from the inevitable bitterness of conflict among former friends' rather than, as some romantics would have it, a 'mysterious substance immanent in social upheaval'.[89] In the case of the Spanish Civil War, the extent to which war and large-scale violence in Spain did not come to an end with Franco's final victory in April 1939 is often forgotten. Historians now estimate that tens of thousands were executed in what Spanish Civil War scholar Helen Graham has called 'the war after the war', as part of an ongoing 'crusade' and campaign of political annihilation directed against members of the former Republican regime and large numbers of its actual and presumed sympathisers.[90] This post-war violence was inextricably connected to the violence of the wartime period, both driven by the 'rebel's ideological imperative'.[91] As historian Michael Richards has written:

> The prolonged intensity of the fighting and of the violence, its viciousness and extensiveness, particularly against non-combatants, and the intractability of the war and the seeming impossibility of negotiation, were all significant as sources of post-war violence. State-building and stability were bound up with total victory and therefore with a continuation of extreme violence.[92]

While the political or ideological element is clear-cut in these two historical cases, political motivations are often difficult to disentangle from other sources of violence, especially at the local and neighbourhood level.[93] Nevertheless, the political content and roots of violence should not be crowded out or dismissed in favour of a primitivisation of violence, a tendency that can be seen in much writing on contemporary conflict.

Perhaps the clearest example of this tendency can be found in German author Hans Magnus Enzenberger's despairing, though powerful and evocative, essay on civil war written against the backdrop of the wars in the Balkans and West Africa in the early 1990s. Enzenberger argues that 'what give today's civil wars a new and terrifying slant is the fact that they are waged without stakes on either side, that they are wars about nothing at all'.[94] This line, in the end, remains deeply unsatisfactory, as the role of crime and criminal violence in civil wars and post-conflict also clearly shows.

Crime and criminal violence

DDR and post-war violence

The effective absence of functioning institutions of law and order and the resulting 'climate of impunity' that often characterises societies emerging from war does much to explain why criminal violence often becomes an endemic part of post-war societies. If, as is usually the case, a formal declaration of peace also involves the release of large numbers of regular and irregular soldiers (sometimes still armed) from military control – either spontaneously or through more-or-less organised demobilisation programmes – into an environment where the opportunities for legitimate income generation and employment are severely restricted, the result is often a sharp increase in levels of criminal violence.[95] The crime spree that followed the end of the civil war in El Salvador was in part a consequence of the fact that soldiers were demobilised over a very short period of time, with the result that some 60,000 guerrillas, soldiers and civil-defence guards found themselves unemployed within one year of the signing of the peace accord.[96] Likewise, the 'flawed dismantling of the Haitian army in 1995, which weakened state authority and filled the slums with disgruntled and well-armed former soldiers', severely compounded by the failure to create a functioning and credible national police force, contributed to the creation of a security vacuum in which levels of crime have risen to extraordinary levels.[97] A 2005 UN study on West Africa found that demobilised soldiers from recent wars had 'joined gangs engaged in trans-border crime in West Africa and beyond', while others had turned 'to armed robbery as a livelihood'.[98] In Iraq, one consequence of the rapid and ill-planned demobilisation of the Iraqi armed forces in May 2003 was a contribution to the unchecked growth of post-invasion criminal violence in Iraq. By one estimate, organised crime accounted for around 80% of the violence in the country in 2005.[99] Some five years after the overthrow of Saddam's regime, '"industrial strength" criminal gangs' were still, according to Toby Dodge, 'the most potent source of violence and instability' in Iraq.[100]

The challenges posed by surplus and demobilised soldiers after war are not, of course, a new phenomenon and the 'relationship of war to crime' is well-established by historians.[101] For example, Julius Ruff, writing on violence in early modern Europe, notes that 'the freeing of soldiers from their military obligations, whether as a result of cessation of hostilities, or of separation from service due to wounds or age, created problems of violence and public order in the early modern period'.[102] Indeed, the kinds of problems generated by demobbed soldiers in early modern Europe bear a striking similarity to those seen in some contemporary post-war settings.[103] One particular characteristic of demobilised soldiers in that period with which there are contemporary parallels was their tendency, remarked on by Ruff, 'to linger around the capital, sometimes demanding back pay and always threatening public order'.[104] Over time, Ruff further notes, the threat posed to civil order by ex-combatants was overcome by improvements in 'military discipline, pay, supply, and housing'; even so, it was a slow and uneven process, and the 'relationship between civilians and soldiers remained fraught with violence'.[105] The post-war crime waves that afflicted Mozambique and Liberia, both concentrated in and around the countries' capitals, were closely linked to flawed and incomplete efforts to reintegrate ex-combatants into an environment characterised by exceptionally high unemployment (estimated at 85% in Liberia in 2003), precious few economic opportunities and the absence of any compensating social safety nets.[106] Other studies have also suggested that demobilised soldiers turning to crime often do so in response to desperate economic hardship.[107]

What of Sierra Leone, where, as remarked above, levels of violence remained comparatively low between 2001 and 2009? The key here appears to lie not so much in the approaches taken to the demobilisation of the rank and file, the success of which has been decidedly mixed, as in attempts made to address the issue of security-sector reform (SSR). Following the crisis of May 2000[108] and the near-collapse of the UN mission in the country, the UK increased its support for a comprehensive SSR programme, committing itself to managing, training and funding reform of both the police and the armed forces of Sierra Leone. This, it has been persuasively argued, had 'a positive impact on the security situation and enhanced the restoration of essential public safety'.[109]

While the verdict on peacebuilding in Sierra Leone must, for reasons discussed more fully below, still be considered tentative, the country's experience of SSR since 2001 does nonetheless highlight the importance of tackling what is clearly a critical challenge to post-conflict stability, above all in the immediate post-war phase: namely, that posed by formations and units associated with the security and military intelligence apparatuses of former belligerents. These come in many guises: special militias, 'self-defence' groups and paramilitary forces, customs bodies and border guards, police units and intelligence outfits of various kinds. In wartime, their ranks swell and their influence grows, just as other law-enforcement bodies – judicial and correctional services – are likely to become politicised, corrupted and unaccountable. Because members of the security sector will have enjoyed a privileged status during the war and, crucially, have had access to instruments of coercion, sources of knowledge and economic resources, they are centrally important to post-conflict stability. Security forces similarly tend to gain in size and influence during periods of authoritarian rule. In the DRC, for instance, Mobutu's long reign saw the creation of an extraordinary number of special paramilitary units, and the leaders of these had every reason to resent the disappearance of the 'Mobutuist system'.[110] The fall of Mobutu in 1997 was not followed by any meaningful reform of the dictator's vast and sprawling security sector, and this accounts in part for the continuing regional instability ever since.

These formerly privileged groups are also critical for another reason: their members often assume a dominant role in organised crime in post-conflict states, though, as hinted above, criminal motives can be difficult to clearly distinguish from political agendas.

Post-conflict peacebuilding and organised crime

The useful broad distinction between criminal activity of an opportunistic kind and more organised forms of criminal behaviour is particularly merited where organised crime within a conflict zone has acquired a transnational character through vertical integration into regional and global criminal networks and illicit markets. However, the distinction is not clear-cut and, indeed, the discussion of 'crime', 'criminal activity' and 'organised crime' in post-war settings poses conceptual and policy challenges that the language of classic law enforcement does not adequately capture.

There are several reasons for this, of which two are particularly relevant to the challenges faced by 'peacebuilders' in post-conflict zones. Firstly, in war-torn societies characterised by extreme levels of socio-economic dislocation, what would in normal circumstances be classified as criminal activity is often impossible to distinguish from 'local survival strategies and coping mechanisms'.[111] As for the notion of 'organised crime' – certainly as it is understood in a classical law-enforcement sense – it fails to recognise 'the complex interpenetration of the legitimate and the illegitimate, the state and crime, that is part of the lived experience of many populations in weak states and conflict-affected areas'.[112] In such contexts, where 'illicit market structures' may be critical to sustaining basic livelihoods, the key assumptions on which the definition of organised crime used in international legal documents rests are problematic.[113] This reality has important and inadequately recognised implications for external actors deployed in a peacebuilding capacity, as they find that organised crime often enjoys a high degree of 'local legitimacy'.[114]

Secondly, not only do levels of criminal 'organisation' vary greatly, but criminal activities often mutate over time into more organised forms. Thus, what may be coping strategies for ordinary individuals and households may eventually be captured by organised crime. Post-conflict environments often provide ideal conditions for facilitating and speeding up this process of mutation. Kidnapping, a distinctive scourge of many post-war settings, is a good example of an activity that has within a very short period of time become highly organised in a number of settings, including Iraq, Haiti, Afghanistan and Colombia.[115]

Even so, though blurred and problematic, the distinction between crime as a coping mechanism and more organised forms of criminal activity is still valid in bringing out what is undeniably an important feature of many modern post-conflict settings: the ability of organised crime to take root and flourish in periods of transition from war to peace, to develop symbiotic relationships with local political elites and to strengthen ties to transnational criminal networks. The UN's 2004 High Level Panel on Threats, Challenges and Change hinted at some of the mechanisms involved, noting how 'in the post-war period, former belligerents seek to exploit criminal connections and know-how developed during the war', and stressing how 'entrenched corruption, the use of violence to protect criminal activities and close ties between criminal enterprises and political elites hinder establishing the rule of law and effective State institutions'.[116]

There are three overlapping reasons why organised crime has become part of so many contemporary post-conflict environments. Firstly, alliances forged between criminal groups and political actors during war have proved remarkably resilient and adaptable, and have often survived into the post-conflict phase. Secondly, post-conflict settings provide attractive enabling environments for organised crime, especially drug trafficking and the criminal trades linked to it such as money laundering. Thirdly, the collapse of communist regimes in Eastern Europe in the early 1990s was in many cases followed or accompanied by the 'privatisation' of state security services (or elements thereof) and this in turn contributed to the emergence of a 'new class of transnational actors'.[117] Often possessing specialist skills and benefiting from technological change and greater economic openness as part of globalisation, in particular the deregulation of industries and services such as transport, these actors have joined and/or facilitated the workings of criminal networks in war zones and post-conflict settings. Each of these three factors merits further discussion.

1. The persistence of wartime alliances

In the absence of reliable systems of revenue collection and logistical support, criminal actors and activities have played a critical role in sustaining the war effort of belligerents in contemporary intra-state conflict, ensuring that critical supplies (notably fuel and arms) and finance have been available to warring parties. Indeed, 'virtually all contemporary wars' of an intra-state kind 'tend to have a criminalised component' for this reason.[118] This is especially true of armed conflicts in which belligerents have not been able to benefit from external patrons for finance and support, as was so often the case during the Cold War. Even where belligerents have had access to natural resources through the control of territory, criminal actors and networks have still been vital for securing access to international markets. Where wartime alliances have been forged between organised crime and belligerents, they have proved difficult to dismantle after the formal end of hostilities and have become integral aspects of the political economy of the armed conflict.

The activities on which criminalised war economies are based revolve around the trafficking and smuggling of a variety of both illicit and licit commodities and goods, from drugs and petroleum products to arms and ammunition. Depending on locality and ease of access to markets they can include cigarettes and a wide variety of natural resources, ranging from gold, gems, oil and timber to rarer metals and strategic minerals. Wartime conditions and the uncertainties of transition from war to peace have also resulted in an increase, at times dramatic, in the trafficking of economic migrants, refugees and women sold into sexual slavery.[119] For example, a UN study of transnational organised crime in West Africa found a 'noticeable increase in human trafficking in Sierra Leone during the war of 1991–2002'.[120] The criminalisation of the economy associated with these activities has in some cases, most notably in the Balkans, been powerfully aided by the imposition of international sanctions and embargos, the effect of which has been to boost informal, extralegal trading networks and create premiums attractive to organised crime.[121] The effects of such policies are often long-lasting. Thus, law-enforcement officials remarked in 2009 how 'the Balkans have ... been identified as a new route [for cocaine] due to pre-established criminal networks set up during the embargo against Milosevic in the late 1990s'.[122] The proliferation of light weapons and small arms and the 'rise of local strongmen' are additional legacies of wartime collaboration between organised crime and belligerent parties.[123]

The dependence of warring factions on relationships forged with organised crime during war has, unsurprisingly, presented external actors with complex 'criminalised legacies for the post-war reconstruction period'.[124] Chief among these is the continuing influence and power of 'war entrepreneurs' and criminal networks after the formal end of hostilities, owing to the close links, in many cases the direct overlap, with members of political and ruling elites. Political scientist Roy Godson has coined the term 'political–criminal nexus' to signify the 'collaboration between the political establishment and the criminal underworld', noting that transition countries and weak states are particularly susceptible to capture by such nexuses.[125] This collaboration, which often cuts across ethnic and sectarian divides, is a feature of many post-conflict environments. It can assume many forms, and the relationship between traffickers and insurgent groups in Afghanistan as described by one Western law-enforcement official follows what seems to be a common pattern: interaction between the groups 'is on a sliding scale of collaboration, cooperation and coercion, based on pragmatic decision, relative strength of forces or leverage, and shared aims for varying lengths of time'.[126]

2. Enabling environments for organised crime

Post-conflict environments offer ideal conditions for certain kinds of organised criminal activity, and this makes them attractive to criminal networks and groups, often from outside the country or region. Antonio Mazzitelli, regional representative of the UN Office on Drugs and Crime for Western and Central Africa, points to the chief reasons for this: 'the permeability of national institutions to corruption, the porosity of borders, the structural deficiencies in states' control of their territories and enforcement of the rule of law' are factors that together exert a strong pull on organised crime.[127] The range of criminal activities and interests in zones of conflict is wide. For example, illegal trade in endangered animals and plants is one of many activities in which criminal networks have become engaged in the eastern DRC.[128] Elsewhere, post-conflict peacebuilding environments that combine 'poorly regulated banking systems, informal cash economies, and a sudden upswing in demand for goods and services paid in foreign currency' have provided ideal conditions for money-laundering activities.[129]

The most significant and lucrative category, however, remains the global industry associated with the production and distribution of opiates, cocaine, cannabis and amphetamines. Over the past 15 years, major developments within the global drugs industry – specifically the consolidation or shifting of supply routes in response to law-enforcement action and the emergence of new transhipment points, 'transit hubs' and cultivation areas – can be explained, at least in part, by the incentives and opportunities for criminal activity that zones of conflict and post-conflict settings have offered. In the Balkans, war and instability allowed the Kosovo Liberation Army to 'consolidate Kosovo as a new centre for the distribution of heroin from Turkey to the European Union', making the now independent republic a key transit point for drugs travelling from Central Asia to Western Europe.[130] In Haiti, mounting instability since the mid 1990s has coincided with the country's emergence as a major transit point, by sea and air, for drugs destined for North American markets; a development which has in turn affected the patterns and sources of violent conflict in Haiti itself. Insecurity and state weakness, resulting in the breakdown of controls in port areas and along borders, have created a highly favourable environment for transnational criminal operations. According to the International Crisis Group, Haiti's 'gang culture has morphed from a primarily community or politically based affiliation where violence was mostly over ideology or turf conflicts, to one increasingly based on crime'.[131] Similarly, West Africa has become increasingly important as a transit zone for international criminal trades and, indeed, the expansion of cocaine trafficking from Venezuela and Colombia to West Africa in 'the last two years [is] possibly the major trafficking route change of the last 30 years'.[132] More than a decade of armed conflict – and with it the explosion of armed groups, the breakdown of institutions of law and order and an overall decline in the quality of governance – has undoubtedly played a key role in this development. The increased use by non-African groups of West Africa as a transit point further indicates that 'the spread of war and the inability of some West African states to offer efficient or effective police services make them attractive as operating bases for criminals from other parts of the world'.[133]

3. New actors and the effects of globalisation
The collapse in the early 1990s of communist regimes in Eastern Europe and the break-up of the Soviet Union into its constituent republics was accompanied by an initial downsizing and a subsequent 'privatisation' of large, often highly specialised, security services and intelligence outfits. Many of those who

had been employed by state security services became part of large criminal networks that thrived and continue to thrive on the conditions created by conflict and the opportunities presented by the rapid opening up of rigid, state-controlled economies. Viktor Bout, a Russian arms dealer who has surfaced in numerous post-Cold War conflicts, is only the best-known example of a new breed of transnational criminal actors who, in the words of one senior official, 'feed upon conflict and post-conflict situations'.[134] The transition from employment with state security services to organised crime was in many cases smooth and, in some, nearly seamless. In Bulgaria and Romania, the security services during the communist era – the Dasharvna Sigurnost, or DS, in the former and the notorious Securitate in the latter – had long been involved in the 'smuggling of drugs, guns, and cigarettes to fund their operations and for personal enrichment'.[135] The Securitate's network in Romania consisted of an estimated 14,000 agents and 500,000 informants.[136] In Bulgaria, between 12,000 and 17,000 state employees of the security services were dismissed between 1990 and 1992 following the passage of a tough 'lustration' law.[137] The disbanding of both the DS and the Securitate led to a massive growth in the private-security industry, which came to include 'many criminal elements'.[138]

Almost by definition, this subject is murky and difficult to research, and it is especially hard to accurately measure the scale, scope and nature of criminal involvement in conflict and post-conflict areas. Enough is now understood, however – thanks in part to UN investigations into sanctions violations in Angola[139] and elsewhere in Africa, court proceedings following successful police investigations, and an improved understanding of the role of the secret police and internal security services in former Eastern bloc countries – to establish this phenomenon as a qualitatively significant factor in the growth of organised crime after the Cold War.[140] It is a factor that has often had direct relevance to stabilisation efforts in zones of conflict. In particular, it is clear that the violent disintegration of Yugoslavia and the sanctions regime imposed on the region created unique business opportunities for organised crime just as ex-Warsaw Pact countries sought to purge and reform their security services.[141] Many of those who were expelled from or otherwise left these services continued to prosper in parts of the Balkans uneasily transitioning from war to peace after 1995.[142] This particular instance may, however, have been a historically unique confluence of factors, and it has been argued, most recently by the UN Office on Drugs and Crime, that the grip of organised crime on southeastern Europe, though still significant, has begun to loosen.[143]

Implications for peacebuilding: combat or accommodation?
The relationship between organised crime and violence in post-conflict settings – especially in the immediate and early post-war phase that is the primary focus of this book – is more complicated than the public pronouncements of policymakers on the subject typically suggest. Such statements, unsurprisingly and not without good reason, emphasise the costs of organised crime, presenting the need to combat and eradicate it as a moral imperative. And yet, as an issue confronting peacebuilders on the ground it has repeatedly presented morally complex dilemmas and policy trade-offs.[144] There are two reasons why an exclusive focus on combating or eradicating organised crime, drawing upon traditional law-enforcement models and categories, has not only met with mixed success but has sometimes threatened to undermine the fragile stability that characterises post-conflict societies in the early phase of external involvement.

In the first instance, and as a more general observation, 'criminal enterprises ... are not invariably negative in their impact on political stability'.[145] In the short term at least, 'participation in informal and illegal economic economies can act as both a safety net and a safety valve for dispossessed populations, proving sources of employment and subsistence that are simply not available in the licit economy, thereby enhancing stability'.[146] The tendency for cooperation in illicit activities and among criminal networks to cut across sectarian and other divides supposedly at the root of a conflict can also contribute to a degree of 'coerced stability', thereby having a positive effect on levels of violence.[147] In some cases, organised crime can even serve to 'facilitate inter-communal exchange and transactions, helping to integrate the economic lives of former adversaries'.[148] Patterns of cooperation among adversaries of this kind are particularly well documented with respect to the Balkans, but are far from unique to this region.[149]

Secondly, the power and authority of criminal groups may be such that confronting them head-on would be likely to prove destabilising, especially if the resources for doing so are limited and the criminal groups enjoy a degree of local legitimacy through their ability to offer services and protection that shore up precarious livelihoods and provide basic security against physical threats.[150] Outsiders may in some cases have few choices but to find a measure of accommodation with illicit power structures, especially where the resources deployed are limited and the commitments short term. In Afghanistan, though public attention in this context mostly focuses on the Taliban's close ties to the illegal drugs industry, 'key governmental, tribal and other figures vital for political stability [also] have vested interests in the drug trade'.[151] In addition, there is a risk that 'in extreme cases, peace operations' actions to stem illicit revenues (such as crop-eradication efforts) may create a backlash demand for protection from these very peacebuilding efforts, playing into the hands of established criminal networks and armed groups consolidating illicit markets.'[152] This has presented a key and divisive dilemma to international forces in Afghanistan.

Against these more pragmatic and short-term considerations, however, must be placed the enormous human cost and misery associated with organised criminal activity, much of it down the chain of exploitation and not immediately visible. In addition to this, 'short-term stability is often purchased at the expense of long-term stability',[153] and it is clear that long-term stability cannot but be undermined by the criminalisation of post-conflict societies. As one senior official working in Afghanistan observed, 'it needs highlighting how crime and instability can limit and strangle any fledgling legitimate businesses in post-conflict environments, which in turn accelerates the descent into a criminal state'.[154]

Given these tensions, setting realistic policy priorities is as important as it is difficult. At the very least, this discussion suggests that efforts to meet the challenge posed by organised crime in post-conflict societies must proceed from a nuanced understanding of the roots and functions of this kind of crime in the local community, including the degree of legitimacy that it may enjoy. All-important in this regard is the need to unravel the relationship of organised crime with 'existing authority structures' within a peacebuilding environment, establishing whether that relationship is 'predatory', 'parasitic' or 'symbiotic'.[155] Such understanding must then feed into the strategy adopted for meeting the challenges posed by crime and criminal enterprises in post-conflict settings. Policy initiatives must also take account of and reflect the actual resources available for addressing the challenges identified, while seeking to minimise the unintended consequences of tackling only a limited aspect of what is necessarily a larger and more multifaceted challenge.

Historically and culturally embedded forms of violence

Exploring the relationship between history, culture and violence is sensitive and fraught with danger. The reason for this is that:

> any allusion to historical patterns of violence risk[s] being misinterpreted as an assertion that violent action is determined by culture, and that culture refers not to repertoires of action whose meaning is broadly understood within a given population but to the habitual thoughts and actions of homogeneous groups of people.[156]

Growing interest, especially since 2003, in the insights that might be offered by cultural anthropology as an aid to military (specifically counter-insurgency) operations in non-Western societies has added to concerns about the 'problem of selective usage and application of anthropological concepts without working through the rather tedious job of uncovering historical context and local specificities'.[157] These are legitimate concerns. That concepts can be invoked superficially and without the necessary groundwork does not mean, however, that, properly used, they cannot make useful contributions to an appreciation of the historical roots and cultural context of contemporary manifestations of violence. Furthermore, such an appreciation is centrally important to an understanding of post-conflict societies. One of the contributions of anthropological works on violence and war has been to stress the need for war 'to be understood in relation to patterns of violence already embedded within society' and, along with this, to recognise that it 'can only be explained by reference to cultural and ideational as well as material factors'.[158] While seeking to do so is not to condone or justify violence, it 'may involve the

hard lesson that violence can have a different kind of legitimacy in other cultures than our own'.[159] In the case of the West
African wars of the 1990s, for example, historian Stephen Ellis
has pointed to:

> [the] revival or reinvention of traditional sodalities
> that once played an important role in governance, that
> are still widely regarded in rural areas especially as
> having socially legitimate rights to inflict or regulate
> violence, and that in current circumstances are being
> reformulated in the form of private armies or militias
> in the service of various national politicians.[160]

Writing about the Algerian civil war in the 1990s, academic
authority on the Maghreb Luis Martinez has argued that the
bloody events of that decade cannot be fully understood without
an appreciation of a deeply rooted 'image of war' shared by
both the military and the armed Islamic groups, according to
which, historically, social advancement has been achieved, and
wealth and prestige obtained, through the use of violence.[161]

There is a related consideration here. Attitudes towards and
forms of violence in societies emerging from war will also be
shaped by the 'complexity of communities' reactions to lived
violence'.[162] That complexity will be determined by the nature
and duration of the armed conflict in question, and the uses
of violence within it. In the case of Guatemala, nearly four
decades of brutal civil war marked by state terror and widespread atrocities targeting civilian populations was followed
by a post-conflict period that has witnessed a dramatic increase
in collective vigilantism in the form of lynchings. Seeking to
account for this phenomenon through ethnographic research,
sociologist Angelina Godoy stresses how during the war
'community life itself – people's way of coming together and

relating to one another, their interactions and expectations – [were] deeply infused with violence'.[163] This, she suggests, provides part of the explanation for post-war levels and types of violence. At the very least, the case of Guatemala confirms what has been identified as a major finding of other ethnographic studies: 'war and violence echo in collective and individual memory for generations'.[164]

Violence has often also played a prominent role in the recent political life and history of some of the societies into which Western forces have intruded, a role that fits poorly with the modern Western conception of violence as strictly regulated and having no place in politics and political processes. Iraq, Haiti and the DRC offer three striking examples of this. One of three themes running through the history of modern Iraq identified by Charles Tripp is 'the use of violence in political life' and its consequences for the nature of the state and politics.[165] In Haiti, ever since independence from France was secured in 1804 following, uniquely, a successful slave uprising, the use of violence – as a way of settling disputes, doing business and maintaining a hold on power – has been central to the political life of the country. In what is now the DRC, violence was a central and regulating principle at the heart of the 'Mobutuist system of institutional theft and corruption'.[166] As development scholar Zoë Marriage has written:

> Seizing and retaining power is associated with direct violence in Congo, and elites have at times deliberately fuelled and exploited insecurity to impose and maintain a particular political order. As leaders arrive and leave with their entourages, armies become rebels and rebels become armies. This affects the formation of political and economic hierarchies, and power is accordingly associated more closely with violence

than with bureaucratic political institutions. The colonial regime, the regime of Mobutu and the rebellions
of the Alliance of Democratic Forces for the Liberation
of Congo (ADFL, led by Laurent Kabila) and the RCD
[Congolese Rally for Democracy] have each demonstrated that force is the means to power.[167]

The overall argument being made here is emphatically not
that certain societies are prone to violence in some primordial
sense and that, consequently, any attempts to create stable, less
violent polities are doomed to failure. Rather, what is clear,
without essentialising violence, is that post-conflict violence in
the countries cited simply cannot be divorced from an understanding of the roles that violence has historically played
within them.

Violence and post-conflict settings

There is a final point to be made on the subject of violence and
insecurity in post-conflict settings. In drawing attention to the
logic and functions of violence that are often hidden behind
the media epithets of 'senseless' and 'chaotic', the observations
above are intended, in part, to counter the tendency to patholo-
gise violence, seeking instead, not to justify or to condone, but
to better understand its sources. Implicit in this is a recognition of the possibility that 'ordinary' people – to borrow the
phrase from historian Christopher Browning's famous work
on the actions of a German reserve police battalion in Poland
during the Second World War – may under extraordinary
circumstances be brutalised and conditioned into committing
deeds of unmitigated horror and evil.[168] That said, the search
for understanding, vitally important as it is, is itself problematic. For example, over the past decade, social-science-based
approaches to understanding violence have often attached great

explanatory power to the strategic and rational calculations that motivate perpetrators of violence. While illuminating and persuasive to a degree, presenting 'human agents as essentially rational actors computing cost-benefit calculations' – especially when done in the context of war and conflict – often involves a gross simplification of human motivation and psychology. Above all, it tends to underplay both the importance of historical context and the 'expressive, emotional and psychological aspects of violence'.[169] Anyone who worked closely on, or even studied from a distance, civil wars in the post-Cold War era will have encountered violence of an extreme and gratuitous kind that cannot be reduced to instrumental considerations, and attempts to do so are often deeply unsatisfactory. The criticism that has been levelled by Michael Burleigh against 'structural' historians of the Holocaust – that they have been 'fastidious in their avoidance of the corporality of mass murder, finding it "incredible" why men should lend themselves to it' – might also be directed against some of the social-science-inspired explanations of violence in civil wars.[170]

The point here is not that the search for understanding should cease, nor is it to suggest that eminently rational calculations do not sometimes play a role in the production of violence. Rather it is to recognise that insecurity and violence in the 'peacebuilding environment' is frequently associated with individuals who, driven by a complex of motivations, thrive during war and will have very little interest in 'sustainable peace'. The reason for this, at one level, is obvious. Post-war environments – marked by state weakness, material shortages, socio-economic dislocations and human suffering – have always been propitious settings for extra-legal and criminal activities, and for the advancement of the careers that go with those activities, not only of the world's Harry Limes – the morally stunted and unscrupulous profiteers on human misery – but also of those, such as Zeljko Raznatovic ('Arkan') in Bosnia, Sam 'Mosquito' Bockarie in Sierra Leone and Joseph Kony in northern Uganda, who have been prepared to inflict suffering of an extreme and horrific kind. In dealing with the challenge such individuals present, policy should seek, at the very least, to avoid actions that will feed back into continued or renewed violence, though this has plainly proved much easier said than done.

The political economy of war and peace

From 'greed versus grievance' to a political-economy perspective on armed conflict

News coverage of the atrocities that accompanied wars in the Balkans and Central and West Africa in the early post-Cold War years – detailing the targeting of civilians, sexual violence and acts of calculated cruelty that seemed to defy any military or strategic rationale – reached governments and publics in the West with the unprecedented speed and penetrative power of modern media. One consequence of this was to reinforce a tendency, especially marked in journalistic reporting of wars in the developing world, to stress the 'essentially inexplicably primordial qualities' of contemporary armed conflict.[171] Perhaps the best-known account along these lines was provided by journalist Robert D. Kaplan, whose coverage of war in West Africa in the early 1990s led him to conclude that a new form of 'criminal anarchy' was emerging as 'the real 'strategic' threat' of our age.[172] This primitivisation of post-Cold War violence was felt by many to be deeply unsatisfactory, and it was one reason why the role of economic agendas in the emergence and perpetuation of civil wars began to attract more systematic attention in the latter half of the 1990s.[173] Interest in the subject was also prompted by the desire to resolve an apparent puzzle: why were long-standing conflicts previously fuelled by Cold

War patronage now proving so resistant to external efforts aimed at bringing them to an end? It was a question that the horrors and history of broken promises in Angola throughout the 1990s seemed to raise with special force and urgency. Part of the answer appeared to lie in evidence – supported by the Angolan case – indicating that warring factions were developing new and increasingly efficient ways of generating their own funds and war material. This 'observable increase in the self-financing nature of combatant activities' provided a major stimulus for work on the economic dimensions of civil wars.[174]

The initial focus of this work centred on the way in which specifically 'rebel' or 'insurgent' groups were financing continued war through the exploitation of natural resources, ranging from minerals and metals to oil, timber and various agricultural products. Such exploitation, as numerous instances made clear, also afforded ample opportunities for personal enrichment and rapacious behaviour. It was these findings that underpinned the so-called 'greed thesis' of civil war, associated above all with the work of Paul Collier during his period as director of the Development Research Group at the World Bank between 1998 and 2003. Writing in 2000, Collier suggested that 'grievance-based explanations of civil war are ... seriously wrong'; the key to understanding why such wars erupted lay instead in greed and calculated plunder by rebel groups.[175] Drawing on statistical data and a rational-choice mode of thinking, still more wide-ranging conclusions were drawn.[176] The likelihood of greed-driven wars erupting was particularly high, it was argued, in countries that relied heavily on the export of primary commodities, had a large surplus of young, unemployed and poorly educated men, and were going through a period of sharp economic decline.[177]

Collier's work provided a welcome spur to the study of the economics underpinning contemporary intra-state wars. It also powerfully informed international policymaking in relation to these wars, especially at the UN, where efforts to curtail trade in 'conflict goods' in Angola, Sierra Leone and the DRC – efforts that included the imposition of Security Council sanctions on non-state actors – can be traced to the widespread acceptance in policy circles of greed- and rebel-centric explanations for civil wars.[178] An important reason for this acceptance was undoubtedly that the 'greed thesis' rested on statistical analysis and a rational-choice-inspired methodology, which had an immediate appeal for policymakers because, by making a 'conceptual distinction' between greed and grievance in order to get at the 'motivations' for civil war and then, for good measure, discounting 'grievance factors' as 'unimportant or perverse',[179] it simplified the complexity of conflict.

The explanatory power initially given by Collier and colleagues to the exploitation of natural resources by rebel groups for purposes of self-enrichment as the principal cause and driver of civil wars – that is, the 'greed thesis' in its pure and original form – was always problematic. One basic difficulty, it soon transpired, concerned the robustness of the statistical evidence and the quality of the data sets from which such sweeping conclusions were being inferred.[180] Indeed, an independent evaluation of the World Bank's research output between the years from 1998 to 2005, while it welcomed the organisation's work on civil wars, also found serious fault with its 'conceptual and empirical frameworks', noting that 'as a result, the regression analysis in these studies cannot be used to support the conclusions that they ostensibly reach'.[181] While these and other problems identified by scholars – including coding errors, selection bias, and the questionable choice and use of proxies – may be no more than 'pedestrian methodological defects'[182] and therefore in principle remediable, there is a much more fundamental criticism to be made of approaches to civil wars that rely so heavily on statistics and rational choice. In the end, these methods amount to 'ascertaining causes of civil war without studying civil wars … to determine the motives of rebels without studying rebels and rebellion'.[183] And indeed, the obvious shortcomings of the initial polarisation of both the academic and the policy debate around 'greed versus grievance' have emerged most clearly from the growing number of historical and qualitative case studies which, partly in reaction to the economic determinism of the greed thesis, have looked more broadly at the political economy of armed conflict.

These studies – which include not only the more familiar cases from West and Central Africa but also cases from, inter alia, Cambodia, Myanmar, Colombia and the Balkans – make it clear that seeing civil war as a fight over lucrative natural resources prompted and driven solely by the predatory designs and actions of greedy, loot-seeking rebels and corrupt governments is as unsatisfactory and incomplete an approach as those explanations that privilege the 'irrational' and supposedly primordial character of conflict.[184] This is not to suggest that economic motives and opportunities are unimportant to an understanding of the dynamics of conflict, as the example of the DRC discussed more fully below plainly illustrates. Their role in a given conflict, however, can only be properly understood in relation to the historical and political context in which that conflict is played out. As social scientist Karen Ballentine, summarising the findings from a series of case studies, has concluded: 'economic incentives and opportunities have not been the only or even the primary cause of these armed conflicts; rather, to varying degrees, they interacted with socio-economic and political grievances, interethnic disputes, and security dilemmas in triggering the outbreak of warfare'.[185] While the same evidence shows that economic factors play a more critical role in sustaining violence once war has broken out and that they influence both the longevity and the character of conflicts, the impossibility of neatly separating economic and political agendas remains.[186] What are of interest to an understanding of the dynamics of armed conflict as well as its post-conflict aftermath are the many ways in which these agendas are connected. It is the attempt to explore these that constitutes, in essence, the political-economy perspective on armed conflict.

What, then, is the relevance of that perspective to an understanding of the post-conflict environment and the challenges it presents for outsiders engaged in peacebuilding?

'Alternative systems of power, protection and profit'

Perhaps the single most important insight offered by the political-economy perspective is that the distinction between 'conflict' and 'post-conflict', between war and peace, is anything but clear cut, and that transitions from war to peace ought to be viewed as involving, in the words of David Keen, 'a realignment of political interests and a readjustment of economic strategies rather than a clean break from violence to consent, from theft to production, or from repression to democracy'.[187] Armed conflict, in other words, should not be treated merely as the violent collapse of a system, but also as the emergence of a new and 'alternative system of power, profit and protection'; one which does not simply disappear with the formal end of hostilities.[188] Such systems are underpinned by distinctive and highly resilient war economies at the heart of which is often a 'perniciously symbiotic relationship between the economic activity and the violence'.[189] Understanding that relationship requires an appreciation of the way in which a wide range of actors within and outside a conflict zone – political and military elites, economic interest groups and external players (including neighbouring powers, firms and transnational corporations),

as well as ordinary people caught up in and dislocated by war
– develop an interest and see functional utility in the continua-
tion of violence and conflict. Thus, while an armed conflict may
appear senseless and anarchic to the disinterested observer and
is undeniably catastrophic in its consequences for society as a
whole, for some individuals and some groups, violence may
prove highly rewarding and profitable. For those for whom
war has not become an end in itself, the socio-economic dislocations it brings in its wake will require new ways of adapting,
coping and, ultimately, surviving in extreme circumstances.
And, as a growing number of local-level or micro-studies have
shown, the very 'process of adaptation and accommodation is
likely to have an impact on the conflict environment itself, as
well as on the future conception of social and political institutions'.[190]

In order to capture this diversity of interests and motivations
among players in war and post-war settings, a conceptually
useful distinction has been drawn between three categories
of actors: conflict 'entrepreneurs', 'opportunists' and 'depen-
dents'.[191]

The first of these refers to those for whom war, because of
the economic and other apparent benefits it brings, such as
power and prestige, has become an end in itself. Such 'entrepreneurs' often form 'elite networks',[192] or alliances of political,
military and business actors, which in turn form symbiotic ties
with criminal networks, including the new breed of transnational criminal actors discussed earlier in the chapter. In the
second category, armed conflict offers opportunities for enrichment and rent that can be exploited. The 'opportunist' group
typically includes local officials and traders, middlemen,
foreign companies and transnational corporations.[193] Finally,
to populations and citizens at the grass roots whose traditional
livelihoods have been destroyed by war – that is, to the majority

of those living within war-affected societies – the functioning of the war economy at the local level will primarily be a matter of 'coping' or, in some cases, just surviving.

It is clearly the case that these categories and distinctions can never fully capture the fluid reality and ever-shifting conditions that exist on the ground. Nonetheless, to outsiders engaged in or contemplating intervention in a peacebuilding capacity they do offer some sense of the processes by which 'alternative systems' and war economies emerge: processes that involve a criminalisation of the economy, radical changes to 'livelihood strategies' among ordinary people and the continual mutation of goals and objectives among parties to the conflict.

There is a further consideration here. Careful attention to the interaction of political and economic agendas among conflict actors sheds light on two other observable tendencies within many contemporary civil wars. Given the blurring of 'war' and 'peace' alluded to above, these are also highly relevant to an understanding of the dynamics of many of the post-conflict societies covered here.[194]

The first of these is the tendency for supposed enemies to join together and form local alliances or 'informal understandings' in order to reap economic and material benefits from a state of war.[195] Engaging in such cooperative behaviour, numerous contemporary armed groups, ostensibly adversaries, have deliberately eschewed costly fighting and decisive engagements. General Douglas MacArthur famously remarked that 'war's objective is victory – not prolonged indecision'.[196] And yet, 'prolonged indecision', not victory, is what belligerents in many contemporary armed conflicts appear to want. The reason for this, as Keen explains, is that, rather than the defeat of an enemy, the 'point of war may be precisely the legitimacy which it confers on actions that in peacetime would be punishable as crimes'.[197] The list of such local alliances, the formation of which often cuts across ethnic, communal and other ascriptive ties, is long: Serbs, Croats and Bosniac forces during the war of 1992–95; Serbs and Albanians within the province of Kosovo since 1999; Khmer Rouge soldiers, Cambodian government officials and Thai military between 1994 and 1997; MPLA 'business elites' and UNITA commanders in Angola throughout the 1990s. In all these cases, economic, but also more plainly criminal, incentives drove 'politically perverse but economically rational alliances'.[198] It needs to be stressed that the aim of such collaborative arrangements is not to reduce suffering among civilian populations caught up in war, and it very rarely has had that effect. On the contrary, these arrangements have often been entered into precisely in order to ensure that predation on and plunder of civilians and vulnerable groups can be carried out more systematically and effectively.

The second tendency, in some ways closely linked to the first, is for armed factions to fracture into smaller groups, formations or militias. This has been a striking aspect of many of the conflicts in which the prospect of economic gain through wartime plunder has played a central role. In such cases, the specific aims of belligerents have tended to mutate, often rapidly. In the case of Liberia, the initial insurrection against the hated and oppressive regime of Samuel Doe in 1989 was soon followed by a proliferation of armed factions, by one estimate as many as eight by 1994.[199] The wars that began in the late 1990s in what is now the eastern DRC (discussed more fully below) were followed by a 'cancerous metastasis of armies and militias'.[200] In large part this was the result of factions and militias becoming 'criminal, money-making enterprise[s]', something which in turn led to 'internal clashes over spoils' and violent competition for trade routes and local markets.[201]

Clearly, the strength of each of these tendencies is not only a function of the salience or otherwise of powerful economic incentives among belligerents and local actors. The organisational structure, ideological cohesion and nature of the leadership of an armed group are all factors that influence its propensity for fragmentation. Similarly, all armed conflicts mutate over time to some degree, as the aims and strategies of warring parties evolve in response to the changing fortunes of war. Even so, the relative strength of both tendencies is often closely connected to economic opportunities and agendas in war and post-war settings. Equally important to note, however, is that these tendencies do not manifest themselves uniformly across front-lines or within a wider zone of conflict: that is to say, cooperation among adversaries and the fragmentation of armed groups may occur in some localities but not in others. This helps to explain the highly localised character assumed by many conflicts. This has obvious implications for external peacebuilding efforts, as it reinforces the importance of paying close attention not just to the 'bigger picture' (that is, to what happens at the central level in capitals and in negotiating forums or 'dialogues' outside the country) but also to local factors and the micro-level of conflict. The history of war and 'peacebuilding' in the DRC, where, by 2009, the UN had been engaged for nearly a decade, illustrates some of these observations.

The political economy of war and peace in the DRC,
1997–2008
The trajectory of the two Congo wars of 'liberation' that began in the late 1990s offers a particularly striking example of the importance that economic agendas can have in shaping the dynamics of both armed conflict and post-conflict peacebuilding. Even in this case, however, the wars should not be reduced to a desperate scramble for natural resources, as they have apparently been in the accounts of some commentators. 'Making sense' of the war requires a much wider political-

economy perspective, one that also takes careful account of historical context and pre-existing patterns of conflict across the region.

The first of the two Congo wars – both of which originated in the populous and resource-rich Kivu provinces in the eastern part of the country – began in late 1996 and ended, temporarily at least, with the overthrow of Mobutu Sese Seko's oppressive and kleptocratic regime by the Alliance of Democratic Forces for the Liberation of Congo-Zaire (ADFL). Led by Laurent-Désiré Kabila and backed by Rwanda, Burundi and Uganda, the ADFL initially targeted the forces of the former Rwandan Armed Forces and the interahamwe militias that had fled to the eastern DRC after the genocide in 1994, before marching on Kinshasa, which fell May 1997, enabling Kabila to install himself as president. The second war erupted in August 1998, by which time Kabila's former allies Rwanda and Uganda had turned against him, lending their support instead to the newly formed Congolese Rally for Democracy (RCD). The Second Congo War saw the direct military intervention in the DRC of no fewer than six African countries: Rwanda, Uganda, Burundi, Namibia, Zimbabwe and Angola, with the latter three now lending their support to Kabila.[202] In theory, a peace process began when a ceasefire was agreed by six regional powers in Lusaka in July 1999, followed soon after by the creation of what was initially a small-scale UN observer mission (the UN Mission in the Democratic Republic of the Congo, MONUC).[203] The 'peace process' culminated in a formal peace accord and power-sharing agreement signed in Sun City, South Africa, in April 2003 by the government, the opposition and the major rebel groups.

In reality, and in the eastern DRC in particular – in the Kivus, Ituri District of Orientale province and even parts of Katanga province – the distinction between war and peace has remained exceedingly blurred, with periods of relative calm punctuated by major flare-ups of violence and large-scale population displacement. Indeed, according to the UN, in parts of the territory, notably the 'Petit Nord' in North Kivu, there has been 'uninterrupted violence for 15 years'.[204] The first national elections since independence in 1960, which took place in July 2006, have had much less of an impact on patterns of conflict in the east than they have in the rest of the country. Thus, a 'recapitulation of main military clashes' in South Kivu over the past 20 months, prepared by the MONUC mission in March 2007, detailed no fewer than 36 such clashes.[205] In January 2008, a new ceasefire was agreed between the main armed groups in North Kivu and the government. By August 2008, however, this too had collapsed, and the eruption of large-scale fighting in the latter half of the year saw a new wave of displacement, killings and the direct involvement of foreign forces. This latest round of fighting pitted government troops and other armed groups supporting or loyal to President Joseph Kabila, notably the Forces Démocratiques de Libération du Rwanda (FDLR), against the 'rebels' of General Laurent Nkunda, a self-proclaimed protector of Tutsis in the eastern DRC who mutinied in 2004, forming the National Congress for the Defence of the People (CNDP) in 2006. In January 2009, Rwandan troops, under intense international pressure to rein in Nkunda, arrested him. At the same time, around 3,000 Rwandan troops entered the eastern DRC and undertook 'joint operations' with the Congolese army, now against the FDLR and 'Hutu rebels', in an operation that, on the face of it, satisfied the long-standing demand of the Rwandan government for the DRC to confront the *génocidaires* who had fled into the eastern DRC after 1994 and had continued to operate there ever since. Rwandan troops were reportedly withdrawn in late February 2009. These latest developments have done nothing to stabilise the situation, and by mid 2009, NGOs reporting from 'front-line areas' described a situation in the eastern DRC which, in terms of fighting, displacement and atrocities, was as grim as it had ever been.[206]

The human cost of a decade of 'neither war nor peace' has been staggering. Based on a series of mortality surveys, the International Rescue Committee estimates that around 3.9 million people died from 'war-related causes' between 1998 and 2004. A further survey, released before the upsurge of fighting in 2008, found that the DRC's 'national crude mortality rate' was unchanged since the organisation's last survey in 2004.[207]

Alongside the civil war in Sierra Leone, the wars that have raged in the DRC since the late 1990s have come to be viewed, more so than any other instance of contemporary armed conflict, as driven by economic agendas, predation and greed. Plainly, this view contains more than a grain of truth. Yet at the same time, to describe them merely as wars over resources is simplistic, for several reasons. To begin with, the initial rebellions were, as academic Stephen Jackson has shown, not grounded in 'explicitly economic motives', but they then 'became successively more and more economic in … scope, means and ends'.[208] An 'economization' of the war took place, as 'conflict actors capitalize[d] … increasingly on the economic opportunities that war … opened up'.[209] As a UN investigating panel concluded in late 2002, the regional conflict that erupted in 1998 spawned 'overlapping micro-conflicts … fought over minerals, farm produce, land and even tax revenues'. Benefiting from these 'micro-conflicts' were 'criminal groups' whose activities ensured that a 'self-financing war economy centred on mineral exploitation' was able to take root.[210] As large-scale fighting returned to the east of the country in late 2008, the pursuit of economic gain and the protection of economic interests clearly provided part of the underlying reason for the resumption of fighting. These motives also explain the presence to an unparalleled degree of the tendencies discussed above: collusion, fragmentation and conflict mutation.

At one point, the RCD, which backed by Rwanda and Uganda had risen up against President Laurent-Désiré Kabila in August 1998, had fragmented into nine factions. This process of militia formation, fragmentation and renewed fighting in the east of the country has continued in spite of local peace deals and an ongoing, supposedly comprehensive, DDR programme, and has enormously complicated efforts aimed at stabilisation and peacebuilding. An internal assessment by MONUC in early 2007 spoke of six 'types of military forces ... currently present in South Kivu; some of them being besieged with internal rivalries and splits'.[211] And in early 2008, a report by MONUC's Natural Resources and Human Rights Unit into the largest and richest cassiterite (tin ore) mine in the country, at Bisiye in North Kivu, concluded that the 'top brass of pro-Kinshasa military, RCD-Goma and Mayi-Mayi' were all 'benefiting jointly from Bisiye's cassiterite ore instead of fighting for it'.[212] The report also noted how 'one of the most striking aspects of the Bisiye mine exploitation is the high level of violence and lawlessness that surrounds its activities'.[213] Another assessment of the economic dimension of the Kivu conflict carried out by a team of UN investigators in March 2008 brought this out clearly.[214] The report's conclusions, which touch on many of the issues covered above, merit quoting at length:

– North Kivu's natural wealth goes beyond the 'mineral ores' and includes also its forest (e.g. red wood, poaching, and the vast charcoal industry) and the access and control of important trading routes.

– The illicit exploitation of the province's wealth is not only the 'privileged field' of the national and foreign armed groups, but in some cases (e.g. the cassiterite exploitation in Bisiye mine) of the hand of [sic] the national army, the FARDC.

– One of the most striking aspects of the resources economy in the Petit Nord is the *level of violence and lawlessness associated with resource exploitation*. As a matter of fact, there is a clear correlation between the illegal exploitation of the natural richness of the province, the presence of armed forces in the areas of natural resource extraction and around the transit routes to and from these areas; and the high occurrence of human rights violations such as forced labor, extortion, arbitrary arrest and arbitrary execution, in these areas. The aggressors act with a high degree of impunity.

– Although this illegal exploitation of the province's natural wealth appears to be an important contributor for the daily subsistence of the armed groups, the natural resources seems to enrich first and foremost a small group of individuals from all sides (members of the national and foreign armed groups, business men linked with these groups, but also members of the national administration and the national armed forces).

– Those who benefit from this illegal exploitation may be reluctant to let their interests go and therefore it seems plausible that many of the economic players in the province may have an interest in maintaining the status quo rather than moving towards sustainable peace and stability in the province.

– This remarkable symbiosis between the vested interests of seemingly opposing factions therefore merits to be investigated further and should be taken into account in the ongoing Goma process.[215]

As this extract makes clear, the history of conflict in the DRC over the past decade – a country of great and diverse mineral wealth, much of it with lootable characteristics[216] – reveals an extreme case of the 'economisation' of war. However, as with other conflicts where economic agendas have played an important part in sustaining violence, at the core of the Congolese wars lie 'grievances', political issues and security concerns. Some of these are directly traceable to the genocide in Rwanda and the subsequent influx into the eastern DRC of extremist Hutu militia members and soldiers of the former Rwandan Armed Forces who had been directly involved in the killing.[217] Others involve long-standing and deep-rooted tensions over access to land, citizenship and ethnicity, the origins of which lie deep in the pre-colonial and colonial, as well as post-colonial, history of the region.[218] One is not, in other words, dealing with a simple 'resource war', but rather with the complex interaction of economic, political and security interests among numerous parties.[219] This interaction has driven the process of war mutation to the point 'where the structural elements that have caused the conflict in 1996 have been replaced by new, local and regional causes of war'.[220]

Implications for peacebuilding

The importance of economic agendas and the resulting political economy of any given conflict vary from case to case. Still, two broad observations of critical relevance to the stabilisation and peacebuilding efforts of outsiders emerge from the discussion above.

Firstly, an appreciation of how economic and political agendas interact is necessary to the identification of deeper and

informal power structures within war-affected societies, sometimes referred to as the 'shadow' or 'dual' state, that is, the
networks of 'privilege and patronage where real power lies'.[221]
Without an understanding of these structures and networks,
outsiders will grope in the dark and their actions will continue
to produce perverse and unintended consequences, at worst
creating structures that encourage and reward continuing
violence.[222] There is a further consideration here: while war
economies are not closed or impervious to outside pressures
and influences, they often possess a logic of their own that
external actors have too often failed to factor into the design of
their own policies. The consequences of this can be profound,
and there are many examples of the actions of outsiders –
however well-intentioned – creating perverse incentives that
have ended up empowering rather than weakening those
with an interest in continued violence. One of these, alluded
to above, was the impact of the economic sanctions imposed
in the 1990s on Slobodan Milosevic's Serbia and Saddam
Hussein's Iraq. In each of these cases, sanctions had the effect,
especially in the short term, of strengthening rather than weakening the leaders' power bases; a development that had direct
consequences for subsequent post-conflict developments in
both countries.[223] Similarly, as Stephen Jackson has observed
in relation to the wars in that country, 'many policies for tackling the resource dimensions of armed conflict risk unintended
negative consequences when they pay insufficient attention
both to the damage they may inflict on the most vulnerable
and to the perverse incentives they may offer for further rent-
seeking by conflict elites'.[224] In the case of Haiti, International
Peace Institute analyst James Cockayne has shown how a series
of international interventions in the 1990s ended up strengthening the power and reach of organised criminality in the
country.[225]

If these examples draw attention to the ways in which policy interventions can be counterproductive, they also, by definition, suggest how policy interventions can be made more effective. A political-economy approach that helps to identify what are complex but not unintelligible structures of incentives and disincentives for continued violence is an important aid for policymakers, enabling, in theory at any rate, a 'stakeholder analysis of conflict' to be undertaken.[226] Where the exploitation of natural resources is involved, for example, such an approach would allow policymakers to 'distinguish between those who exploit resources for war, those who exploit war for resources, and those, largely civilians, who participate in illicit economic activity as a matter of survival'.[227]

The second observation emerges not only from the discussion of the political economy of armed conflict but from all the contextual categories explored in this chapter. As Susan Woodward reminds us: 'wars are transformative', and 'creating a sustainable peace requires addressing the reality created by that war'.[228] The implications of this for outsiders are profound in two senses. Firstly, recognising the reality created by war may involve jettisoning long-cherished policy prescriptions and a 'templated' approach to peacebuilding. The failure to do just this has been the focus of recurring criticism of the Bretton Woods institutions' involvement in conflicts, especially in the 1990s, when the strictures of structural-adjustment policies – rapid liberalisation, privatisation and the cutting of public expenditure – were advocated seemingly irrespective of context. Secondly, and more subtly, it requires an understanding of the – often unexpected – ways in which a war has transformed social, economic and political relationships on the ground, especially at the local level. As political scientist and Congo specialist Timothy Raeymaekers has written of the DRC: 'During the war, people – farmers, transborder traders, street vendors, but also customs agents, administrators, rebels and commanders of foreign armies that occupied vast parts of Congo's territory – continued to seek and find practical responses to the daily problems of political order under conditions of conflict and state "collapse", a quest that sometimes produced elaborated systems of "governance"'.[229] And yet, as he adds, 'over the past decade, the international community has tried to ... contain the excesses of Congo's ongoing conflict ... without acknowledging the profound transformations of its political system that occurred during and as a result of the war'.[230] As will be explored further in the next chapter, this shortcoming is not unique to peacebuilding efforts and interventions in the DRC.

CHAPTER TWO

Peacebuilding Operations and the Struggle for Legitimacy

The focus of this chapter is on the immediate challenge of peace consolidation and stabilisation that confronts an outside force deployed in a peacebuilding capacity. It was stressed in the Introduction that this period cannot be defined in simple temporal terms, nor should it always be associated *merely* with risk or danger. It is better viewed as a *critical* phase of uncertain duration, a unique kind of political space distinguished by that potent and 'volatile mixture of euphoria and anxiety about the future' of which Isam al-Khafaji spoke in relation to Iraq. That said, and whatever the level of euphoria, the period is typically also characterised by a widespread sense of insecurity, by continuing violence and by the weakness, or even the absence, of legitimate and properly functioning institutions, especially in the area of law and order. As a consequence, distinctions between 'war' and 'peace', 'conflict' and 'post-conflict' tend to be blurred and unclear.

Against this backdrop any outside force is faced with three broad priority tasks, all of which require simultaneous attention if progress is to be made in the other areas covered by the UN's more expansive definition of peacebuilding: providing a secure environment; stabilising governing structures; and ensuring the uninterrupted flow of basic, life-sustaining services. These are all, of course, intimately connected: addressing basic needs requires a measure of security, while security itself is closely tied to the stability and perceived legitimacy of institutions of governance within an area of operation, whether those institutions are formal or informal, properly institutionalised or more spontaneous and grassroots based. In other words, the enumeration of these priorities does not imply a sequential approach to tasks to be taken by outside actors: they are mutually reinforcing and need to be pursued in parallel. As Hilary Synnott observed of his time in southern Iraq, 'there was an inextricable linkage between the security environment, progress over governance and reconstruction, and public perception'.[1] That linkage exists in all 'post-conflict' settings.

Stated in such broad and abstract terms, these priorities appear self-evident. Each of them, however, raises new and more searching questions and the answers to these – judging by the post-Cold War record of peacebuilding as a whole – have proved anything but clear-cut or self-evident. What role should military force and armed forces play in efforts to establish a secure environment so that other peacebuilding objectives can be pursued? Does a more careful balance need to be struck in the early phase of operations between, on the one hand, shoring up and building formal institutions of government and, on the other, encouraging and working with the grain of local, or 'bottom-up', governance initiatives? What is the most efficient way of ensuring that basic services are provided? These are the key questions addressed here. Addressing them, however, requires a preliminary discussion of the fundamental approach or operational mindset that *any* outside force must bring to the job of laying the initial foundations for lasting peace in societies ravaged and traumatised by war.

Legitimacy, security and peacebuilding

Imposing or eliciting stability?

If there is one overarching lesson to be drawn from the decidedly mixed record of post-conflict interventions since the early 1990s it is that stability cannot be imposed on war-torn societies from the outside. It has, in Synnott's phrase, to be 'elicited'.[2] In part, this is because political will among external actors is limited, and there is no appetite for the kind of open-ended commitment that an attempt truly to impose peace would require. Notwithstanding the rhetoric that has accompanied many peacebuilding endeavours, even those states most supportive of the 'new interventionism'[3] have rejected suggestions that it amounts to a new, more benign, form of empire-building. The de facto UN protectorates set up in Kosovo and East Timor were always intended to be temporary and, as the difficulties of transforming societies by means of external manipulation have become ever more apparent, so have the challenges, especially for Western governments, of shoring up domestic political support for commitments of uncertain duration and uncertain outcome. But just as importantly, as far the difficulty of imposing stability is concerned, careful consideration of the contextual categories examined in the previous chapter will, invariably, reveal the limits on what can be imposed from the outside. How, then, is stability to be elicited?

The key lies in the notion of legitimacy. The theme of legitimacy – how to conceptualise it, how to pin down its elusive quality – is of course central to the study and theorisation of politics. For the more limited purpose of the argument here, political scientist Ian Hurd offers a helpful definition of the concept as 'the normative belief by an actor that a rule or institution ought to be obeyed ... a subjective quality, relational between actor and institution, and defined by the actor's perception of the institution'.[4] He elaborates: 'When an actor believes a rule is legitimate, compliance is no longer motivated by the simple fear of retribution, or by a calculation of self-interest … control is legitimate to the extent that it is approved or regarded as "right".[5] In other words, legitimacy is not a fixed quantity of which one is either in possession or not, and in any society – in any relationship between rulers and ruled – it will coexist to some degree with coercion or self-interest as 'modes of social control'.[6] It springs from, and is influenced by, a variety of sources and, crucially, when effectively cultivated, it translates into authority. The relevance of these seemingly abstract considerations to the central focus of this chapter – that is, the activities and priorities of external actors in the early post-conflict phase – should be obvious. Legitimacy is vital in two, closely related, respects.

Two kinds of legitimacy in post-conflict settings

There is in the first instance the perceived legitimacy of the outside force itself, a function of its conduct, identity and ability to meet local expectations. The success of any post-conflict intervention – whether it follows a coercive intervention as in Iraq after 2003, is in support of a negotiated peace accord as in Bosnia and Cambodia, or is designed to shore up a fledgling peace operation as in West Africa – requires constant attention to the legitimacy-enhancing effects or otherwise of its actions. Building legitimacy should serve as the lodestar for an external force, a guiding principle exercising a continuous influence on the activities of both the military and civilian sides of a mission. The importance of this cannot be overstated, a fact to which numerous attempts over the past two decades to stabilise war-afflicted societies bear testimony. The fortunes of the different formations of the US army in Iraq after 2003, especially during the first year of occupation, illustrate the point with particular clarity.[7] Indeed, in the view of some observers, 'the insurgency was substantially created by the tactics used by the occupying force' during that early period.[8] Although the force was initially welcomed by segments of the population, 'ambitious generals, who should have known better, created a very aggressive do-what-is-necessary culture', while 'frustrated troops, with no familiarity with the language or culture, naturally [made] mistakes'.[9] In a similar vein, Toby Dodge emphasised in testimony to US lawmakers in 2004 how 'the repeated violations of the private sphere of Iraqi domestic life by US troops searching for weapons and fugitives ha[d] caused recurring resentment across Iraq, especially when combined with the seizure of weapons and money'.[10] While the early experiences of US forces in Iraq offer a particularly stark example of how support can seep away from an intervening force, cultivating legitimacy is no less important in more permissive operational environments where the consent of local populations is, at least initially, more broad-based and unequivocal. The reason for this is that the 'legitimacy of any intervention', however well-intentioned, is 'never … secure'.[11] During UNTAC's operation in Cambodia from 1992 to 1993, contingents from Bulgaria, Tunisia and Indonesia were felt by many to have undermined the credibility of the UN mission in the eyes of ordinary Cambodians.[12] Similarly, the reputation of the Economic Community of West African States Monitoring Group (ECOMOG) in Liberia in the mid 1990s was badly damaged by the involvement of Nigerian troops in systematic looting and corruption.[13] More recently, the revelations of sexual exploitation and abuse 'by a significant number of UN peacekeeping personnel in the DRC' have, by the secretary-general's own admission, 'done great harm to the name of peacekeeping'.[14] Subsequent allegations, many of them since substantiated, about the involvement of Pakistani and Indian troops in gold smuggling and arms trading in the eastern DRC have further tarnished the standing and credibility of MONUC, rendering the task of peacebuilding all the more challenging.[15] All of these cases point to a wider lesson: while building legitimacy is a demanding and painstaking process the effects of which are difficult to measure, undermining and destroying it can be accomplished quickly, sometimes with irreparable consequences.

The second understanding of legitimacy in post-conflict settings has to do with the structures of governance that an outside force helps to implant, nourish and consolidate. Put simply, the relative success of peacebuilding interventions depends not only on the conduct and actions of outsiders in the theatre of operations, but also on the degree to which the governance structures put in place and promoted by outsiders command legitimacy in the eyes of local parties, neighbouring states and the wider international community. This second, plainly related, understanding of legitimacy in post-conflict settings will be discussed more fully below.

Stated in these terms, the importance of legitimacy appears obvious enough and, indeed, is frequently acknowledged in mission statements. The central implication, however, has often been neglected, namely that both the planning and the pursuit of priority tasks set out above should *at all times* be driven by an overriding concern with the cultivation and maintenance of this double legitimacy.

The search for security: the use and utility of force in peacebuilding operations

The challenge of establishing a peacebuilding environment that is sufficiently secure and predictable for longer-term objectives to be pursued without fear of sudden and catastrophic reversal inevitably raises the issue of the use and utility of military force. The fact that 'peace operations', especially in their early stages, are frequently confronted by 'spoilers' of various kinds has meant that the question of what constitutes a prudent and appropriate military response to threats – whether to a mandate or even to a mission as a whole – is never far from the surface.[16] It is not surprising, therefore, that it was a key question for the 2000 Brahimi Panel on UN Peace Operations; a panel whose overriding concern was to ensure that the peacekeeping failures of the 1990s – in Somalia, the former Yugoslavia and, above all, Rwanda – were not repeated.

Those failures had raised two broad and intertwined issues. The first concerned the capabilities and resources required to meet unforeseen challenges in non-permissive and dangerous environments. While the traditional principles governing UN peacekeeping operations – consent, impartiality and minimum use of force except in self-defence – were found by the panel to be 'generally valid' in the 'context of intra-State/transnational conflicts', these same principles were also, as the 1990s showed, dangerously susceptible to manipulation by the parties to a conflict. To counter this, the Brahimi report called for 'bigger forces, better equipped and more costly but able to be a credible deterrent'.[17] In hostile settings, the uncertainties that have plagued even the most benign of UN operations – uncertainties related to speed of deployment, readiness and unity of effort, unity of command, information-gathering and management, tactical mobility, force protection – are multiplied many times over. The Brahimi report offered innovative suggestions to address these weaknesses and a number of these have been acted upon.[18]

The Brahimi panel did not, however, suggest that the predicament in which UN forces repeatedly found themselves in the 1990s was attributable merely to a lack of resources. Ultimately, the success or otherwise of any operation depended on 'clear, credible and achievable mandates'.[19] Without these, a mission would always be vulnerable to manipulation by spoilers and

constantly at risk, in some cases with catastrophic consequences.

The broad conclusions of the Brahimi panel – relating, on
the one hand, to the resource base and capabilities of an outside
force and, on the other, to its mandate, specifically its political
direction and sense of strategic purpose – remain fundamentally valid and apply to all 'peace operations', not merely those
under the auspices of the UN. A force that is ill-equipped, logis-
tically over-stretched and lacking in deterrent capacity will – as
the experience of the UN Mission in Sierra Leone (UNAMSIL)
in the 'crisis' of May 2000 showed all too clearly – always be
operationally hamstrung and vulnerable to forceful challenges.
At the same time, the capabilities and resources at the disposal
of an intervention force – as other non-UN operations, notably
NATO-led efforts Afghanistan since 2003, have clearly demonstrated – cannot by themselves substitute for clarity of overall
strategic purpose and a clear sense of political direction.

Lessons from Sierra Leone, the eastern DRC and Haiti

Merely reiterating the lessons from Brahimi will, however,
only take us so far. There is a simple reason for this: the history
of UN peace operations since 2000 has shown that resource
constraints will never be fully overcome and that a perfect
clarity of mandate will always prove hard to obtain, even for
missions where the operational environment is comparatively
benign and the political end-state more clear-cut. It is in the
light of this more messy reality that the question of the use and
utility of military force in operations must be considered. With
a view to examining this reality, three operations from the past
decade merit attention for the range of lessons – both positive
and cautionary – that they offer: *Operation Palliser*, deployed to
deal with the rapidly deteriorating situation in Sierra Leone in
the spring of 2000; *Operation Artemis* and its aftermath in the

eastern DRC after 2003; and the UN operation to confront the urban gangs and armed groups that threatened to overwhelm Haiti in 2006–07.

Operation Palliser in Sierra Leone

In early May 2000 the Lomé peace accord for Sierra Leone was finally and cruelly exposed for what it was: 'a slapdash peace agreement that turned out not to exist except on paper'.[20] UNAMSIL, the UN peacekeeping force sent to the country to help implement the agreement, was at the point of collapse, its parlous state revealed by its vulnerability following the final withdrawal of ECOMOG troops from Sierra Leone in late April. Overstretched, ill-equipped and ill-prepared for combat, UNAMSIL was reeling from RUF attacks and mass detentions of its personnel, leaving its credibility in ruins.[21] This credibility was not helped by the posture initially taken by UN peacekeepers, even though UNAMSIL had only been 'designed, equipped and deployed as a peacekeeping force'.[22] Brian Urquhart, a former senior UN official and long-term observer of the UN and its history, put it bluntly: UN troops 'were extremely unimpressive at exactly the moment when they most needed to give the impression of confidence and military superiority'.[23] With UN and government forces in retreat, Brigadier David Richards, commanding the British force about to deploy to the country, detected 'a palpable fear amongst the locals that they were about to be subjected to a repeat of the RUF attack on Freetown the previous year'.[24]

It was in response to these events that, beginning on 7 May, the UK dispatched combat troops to Sierra Leone in *Operation Palliser*. At the operation's peak in mid June 2000, nearly 4,500 UK personnel were deployed, including some 1,350 ashore.[25] Sent in the first instance to assist in the evacuation of British nationals, the troops ended up providing an effective deterrent against another rebel assault on Freetown and, more generally, helping to shore up the faltering UN mission, both by 'encouraging the UN to fight' and, crucially, by making the Sierra Leone Army into a more 'effective fighting force'.[26] The operation actually saw very little fighting. Still, a few brief fire-fights, including near the airport, had 'immense psychological effect'.[27] According to Richards, 'the most decisive factor was persuading General Jetley [the Indian UNAMSIL force commander] to move from a peacekeeping to a conventional defensive posture, and convincing him that [the] RUF were not supermen'.[28]

There is no doubt that the deployment of British troops in May 2000 and their manifest readiness to use force played a key role in preventing the collapse of the UN operation and a return to full-scale war. As the UN secretary-general acknowledged at the time, the troops' arrival had been 'a pivotal factor in restoring stability'.[29] Highly capable ground troops accompanied by a 'substantial naval presence offshore' had 'boosted [the] confidence of Sierra Leoneans, and enable[d] UNAMSIL to redeploy much-needed troops to areas east of Freetown'.[30] This confidence-boosting capacity was demonstrated again in September following the capture of 11 British soldiers by the pro-AFRC faction known as the 'West Side Boys', whose members had played a major role in the horrific attack on Freetown of January 1999.[31] The decisive military action taken on 10 September (code-named *Operation Barras*) to secure the release of these hostages, who had been engaged in training the Sierra Leone Army, proved in retrospect to be particularly timely, as it helped to mitigate the negative psychological effects of India's decision to withdraw from UNAMSIL later that month and to avert the loss of the force's credibility this might have prompted.[32]

Since 2002, Sierra Leone has provided a welcome and positive contrast to many of the other post-conflict settings examined in this study. While the reconstruction challenges ahead are still formidable and the wounds of war have yet to heal, levels of violence have remained comparatively low and a return to full-scale war is considered very unlikely. The presidential and parliamentary elections of August 2007 passed off remarkably successfully and were followed by the orderly transfer of power to a new government. The contrast with developments in Central Africa and the Horn of Africa over the same period is particularly striking. It is no doubt partly for this reason that the UK intervention and its robust use of force in May and August 2000 have been widely identi-fied – not least by the British themselves, whose subsequent involvements in Iraq and Afghanistan have been more divisive and less conclusive – as a crucial 'tipping point', the decisive factor that finally put Sierra Leone on the path of recovery and sustainable peace.

While *Operation Palliser* clearly did play a crucial role in restoring stability at a critical moment, thus reinforcing the major conclusions of the Brahimi report, the operation's significance should be balanced against the contribution and relative importance of other factors to the final outcome. What Hew Strachan notes of the Malayan campaign between 1948 and 1960 seems also to fit the 'story' of *Operation Palliser*: 'it has probably improved with telling'.[33] Regarding the central question about the use and utility of force in peacebuilding or peace operations, there are three issues here that merit special attention.

First, the British military intervention was only one factor contributing to the weakening of the RUF – the principal spoiler and threat to UN peacebuilding efforts – and the eventual emer-gence of that force's grudging acceptance of a UN peacekeeping presence. 'First and probably most important' in influencing these developments, in the assessment of David Keen, 'was the role of Guinea and fighters based there', reportedly aided by Ukrainian mercenaries and private military firms.[34] In April and May, a 'combined assault from Guinean forces and Sierra Leonean civil defence forces dealt a severe blow to the RUF', and raids across the border from Guinea took a 'heavy toll' on RUF commanders.[35] These military setbacks and pressure also had the effect of accentuating existing splits within the RUF between its Eastern and Northern commands.[36]

Second, and crucially important in terms of the long-term outcome, was the UK's decision to follow up a short-term and carefully circumscribed military intervention with immediate diplomatic action, galvanising others to contribute to a reinforced and reconfigured UN mission, while at the same time making a long-term commitment to restructuring Sierra Leone's armed forces and security sector and becoming its largest bilateral donor.[37] Of particular importance, not least psychologically, was the long-term commitment to taking a leading role in training the new Sierra Leone Army. Initially made by the British Military Advisory and Training Team and, from 2002, by the International Military Advisory and Training Team, this commitment was undertaken until 'at least 2010'.

Third, the utility of the military action taken in 2000 must, in the final analysis, be assessed in terms of its longer-term political impact and not merely with reference to its short-term effect on the operational environment. In this respect, the final verdict on Sierra Leone is still open. While real progress has been made, for all the achievements to date, there is still a widespread perception among former rank-and-file soldiers in Sierra Leone that the grievances that led to the outbreak of violence in the early 1990s have yet to be addressed, in particular the 'persistence of informal patronage systems' that continue 'to cause their economic marginalisation'.[38] This feeling, combined with the country's severe economic dislocation, is beginning to translate into greater levels of crime and politically motivated violence, as evidenced by the unrest of March 2009.[39] In addition, as noted in the previous chapter, protracted armed conflict in West Africa has raised the region's role in and importance to organised crime over the past 15 years and concerns are now growing that the comparative success of peacebuilding efforts in Sierra Leone is increasingly under threat from the country's enmeshment in the international drugs trade and the power of the South American cartels that control it.[40]

Operation Artemis and after

With the signing of a 'Global and All-Inclusive Peace Agreement' in Pretoria in December 2002, the Second Congo War technically came to an end.[41] As we have seen, however, in large parts of the eastern DRC – above all in Ituri, North Kivu and South Kivu – 'violence continued unabated as "residual" or "illegitimate"'.[42]

In early May 2003, fighting intensified between Lendu and Hema militias in the Ituri District of Orientale province over control of the regional capital Bunia, following the withdrawal of Ugandan troops that had been deployed there in support of local militias for much of the Second Congo War. The flare-up in fighting saw hundreds of civilians killed, widespread atrocities and large-scale population displacement. As in Sierra Leone three years earlier, UN troops found themselves overstretched, ill-equipped and badly in need of reinforcements. Unable to do much more than secure the UN compound in Bunia, a Uruguayan battalion that had hastily redeployed from elsewhere in the DRC proved unable to cope with the rapidly deteriorating situation, notwithstanding acts of great bravery by individual peacekeepers.[43] On 12 May, Bunia was captured by the Hema-based Union of Congolese Patriots, the most powerful of the numerous armed groups operating in Ituri at the time. The group was led by Thomas Lubanga, who was heavily implicated in massacres that had taken place elsewhere in the district the previous year. In January 2009, Lubanga would become the first person ever to be indicted by the new International Criminal Court in The Hague.

It was against this alarming backdrop that UN Secretary-General Kofi Annan asked the Security Council in mid May 2003 for a 'well-equipped multinational force, under the lead of a Member state' to be deployed to Bunia to provide security and protect civilians.[44] Having first established that France would take the lead and act as the 'framework nation' for an EU force, on 30 May 2003, the Security Council authorised the deployment of an Interim Emergency Multinational Force (IEMF) to Bunia.[45] The force's task would be to 'contribute to the stabilization of the security conditions and the improvement of the humanitarian situation in Bunia … ensure the protection of the airport, the internally displaced persons in the camps in Bunia and, if the situation requires it, … contribute to the safety of the civilian population'.[46] Under the name of *Operation Artemis*, the IEMF deployed to Bunia in early June and remained strictly confined to the town for the duration of its deployment. It was the EU's first autonomous operation outside Europe and the force withdrew promptly, as originally envisaged, in early September 2003, passing on its responsibilities to a newly created and much larger 'Ituri Brigade' of MONUC, which had an authorised strength of close to 5,000 military personnel.[47] At its peak, the IEMF numbered nearly 1,500 military personnel, including the staff at its force headquarters in Uganda.

At the time of deployment and immediately after it, *Operation Artemis* was widely hailed as a 'success'[48] and, in the short term, the EU-led intervention did unquestionably have a significant impact on the local balance of power. It helped to re-establish security in Bunia, using overwhelming force whenever threatened and on occasion doing so pre-emptively.[49] Although the IEMF made no attempt to demilitarise the town, declaring it instead a 'weapons-invisible' zone, militias were driven out and the flow of military supplies from outside was effectively, if temporarily, restricted, something that was made possible by the IEMF's sophisticated and high-tech capabilities for monitoring supply routes (including hidden airstrips) and the movement of forces in the surrounding area.[50] In terms of shoring up the UN's precarious position and serving as bridging force before the expansion of MONUC, the secretary-general later acknowledged that the 'presence of a robustly equipped force in Bunia, under Chapter VII of the Charter, [had] helped to stave off an impending humanitarian crisis'.[51] By the end of the IEMF's mission, the deployment of MONUC's Ituri Brigade was well under way. All of this nourished the hope in some quarters that *Operation Artemis* had set a precedent for future and more robust EU 'autonomous operations' in support of the UN, possibly providing that organisation with a 'strategic reserve' and the 'rapid-reaction capability it sorely needs'.[52]

However, *Operation Artemis*'s claim to 'success' requires serious qualification – much more so than does that of *Operation Palliser* – not only in terms of the operation's longer-term impact on the dynamics of conflict in the eastern DRC, which now looks distinctly limited, but also – though the two are inextricably linked – in terms of its more immediate impact.[53] Because of this, the operation can offer some important lessons about the utility and use of force in peace operations, and for that reason it merits more detailed analysis.

To begin with the mission's immediate impact, *Artemis* was presented and welcomed at the time of its deployment as an example of 'active impartiality', a notion that had been elaborated in 1995 in the aftermath of *Operation Turquoise* in Rwanda by French doctrine staff who had stressed the need for a new category – *'restauration de la paix'* – that would reflect 'more accurately the nature of operations before a conflict has ended and [be] intended to restore peace or moderate the conflict by methods that involve both securing the parties' consent and constraint'.[54] The element of 'constraint' might well involve 'coercive military action', for which an appropriate force must be prepared, trained and equipped. There is, in the abstract, a compelling logic to the concept of 'active impartiality', and its articulation in the mid 1990s must be understood in part as an effort to highlight the limitations – in situations where there is no peace to keep – of 'traditional' peacekeeping practices and, perhaps even more so, of the operational mindset that went with those practices.[55] The Brahimi report sought to do much the same and the early phase of MONUC, from 1999 to 2003, when UN troops were deployed as a 'traditional peacekeeping force reminiscent of the Cold War era', only confirmed the lessons of the 1990s.[56]

And yet, while there is no doubt that 'traditional' principles are deeply problematic in conditions of civil war, the fundamental difficulty of and wider risks associated with the notion 'active impartiality', however compelling the notion may seem on the conceptual drawing-board of doctrine writers, was plainly revealed in Bunia. The difficulty is simply stated: while an intervening force may insist that its activities are truly impartial and take every measure possible to reinforce that message, the local impact of its actions will never be neutral in its political and military consequences. The impact of the actions of outsiders, especially the use of military force, on the perceptions and relative strength of local actors and belligerents will always vary greatly under conditions of ongoing conflict. And it is precisely this impact on the perceptions and relative power position of local actors that will most critically determine the dynamics of conflict and the prospects for stability in the long run. The suggestion here – it needs to be stressed – is *not* that 'coercive military action' of the kind displayed in *Palliser* and *Artemis* is bound to prove inconclusive or even destabilising and therefore should always be ruled out. It is rather that its strategic impact, and therefore its true effectiveness in terms of stabilising a 'peacebuilding' environment, depends crucially on what follows the short-term tactical engagement. Unless this is properly appreciated, it is certainly fair to conclude, as observers have, that it is 'not clear that the occasional robust foray will do the trick'.[57] The experience of *Operation Artemis* underscores this caution. As the head of MONUC's office in Bunia at the time of the deployment, Alpha Sow, later made clear:

> The time and space limit imposed by its mandate … has greatly limited the IEMF military reach, and finally its long-term effectiveness. The force has not been able to extend its action beyond Bunia … The IEMF has thus greatly weakened the UPC, the Hema militia settled within its area of responsibility, without being able to neutralise the UPC's enemies. This has indirectly tilted the balance of power on behalf of the Lendu militia, who were unwittingly allowed free action in several areas of the district, from where they could attack the already weakened Hema strongholds, and take revenge for years of joint Hema/UPDF attacks … While Bunia may be enjoying relative security, the names of towns such as Drodro, Largo, Nizi, and Fataki have become sadly famous for the atrocities committed there against civilians.[58]

In other words, and as a 'lesson learned' report from the UN's peacekeeping department concluded in October 2004, 'the strict insistence on the very limited area of operations – Bunia

– merely pushed the problem of violent aggression against civilians beyond the environs of the town, where atrocities continued'.[59] By late 2004, the situation in Ituri had again deteriorated, which brings us to the question of the wider, long-term significance of *Operation Artemis*. There are two issues here. The first concerns the way in which the UN has increasingly been drawn into the DRC's civil wars; the second, the possible or hoped-for precedent-setting role of *Artemis* alluded to above.

The inability of the UN to operate effectively in a peacekeeping capacity between 1999 and 2003, glaringly exposed during the Ituri crisis that precipitated the IEMF deployment, led to a strengthening of the mandates of MONUC and its incoming Ituri Brigade. Security Council Resolution 1483, passed in late July 2003, mandated an increase in the size of the overall force and explicitly authorised MONUC 'to use all necessary means to fulfil its mandate in the Ituri district and, as it deems it within its capabilities, in North and South Kivu'.[60] The intention was to give the UN more scope for proactive action, allowing it to exercise the kind of 'active impartiality' in defence of the mandate that the IEMF had displayed on much a smaller scale and within strictly defined geographical limitations. The change in mandate and the expansion of MONUC did, notably from 2005 onwards, lead to a much more robust stance and has involved UN troops in 'collaborative combat operations'[61] alongside the new DRC army, the Forces Armées de la République Démocratique du Congo (FARDC), a supposedly integrated force created following the peace accord of 2003. The readiness to use force more offensively was especially marked between 2005 and 2007 when Dutch General Patrick Cammaert served as MONUC force commander in the eastern DRC. Cammaert insisted that his forces were 'not neutral but impartial'[62] and, on occasion, MONUC's aggressive use of force has had a decisive tactical impact, playing, for example, 'a crucial role in preventing Nkunda's capture of Goma in November 2006'.[63]

MONUC's greater readiness to use force has, however, had unintended consequences on a larger scale. In the absence of clear strategic direction, facing a multiplicity of overlapping, often highly localised, conflicts and with a force that remains – notwithstanding the enlargements that have taken place – ill-equipped and under-resourced for the complexities confronting it, MONUC has been drawn ever more deeply into the continuing conflicts in the DRC's eastern provinces. There are two related aspects to this, both of which have enormously complicated the UN's peacebuilding operation.

Firstly, while MONUC has been mandated to operate in support the FARDC, aligning itself with and working alongside the new Congolese army has weakened its legitimacy and indirectly complicated the overall task of stabilisation. While 'more robust tactics' in Ituri from late 2004 onwards may have 'improved the security situation',[64] these improvements plainly came at a high price. According to Joshua Marks, an Africa specialist at the National Endowment for Democracy who was based in the eastern DRC in 2004–05, 'during anti-militia operations in Ituri in 2005–2006, FARDC abuses were especially corrosive to MONUC's image and local support', as the army 'systematically pillaged homes and abused citizens under the pretext of hunting for rebels'.[65] This kind of action has fed into a further dynamic: militias have responded to more aggressive operations by MONUC and the FARDC by stepping up their own predatory activity against civilian populations.[66] At the same time, MONUC, under-resourced and overstretched, has not been able to protect civilians from attack. It is a vicious pattern that has been repeated since and helps to account for the 'catastrophic' situation prevailing in the eastern DRC, where close to half a million people have been displaced since the beginning of 2009.[67]

In December 2008, the FARDC began military operations against the Lord's Resistance Army in Uganda in northern DRC, followed up in January by operations in the eastern DRC (undertaken jointly with Rwanda) against Hutu militias organised in the FDLR. In the second of these, known as *Kamia II*, MONUC has worked closely with the Congolese army, assisting it with logistical and planning support. In the wake of these operations, however, the UN stands accused of both failing to mitigate the humanitarian consequences of the offensives and of aligning itself with government forces that are themselves deeply tainted by atrocities and human-rights violations.[68] This has severely undermined MONUC's legitimacy in the eyes of both local populations and the outside world, and has compromised its wider peacebuilding role. As one official privately observed in July 2009, 'it does appear that MONUC is hopelessly and helplessly, yet seemingly inexorably, being drawn into another civil war'.[69] While the UN has responded by taking a harder line with the FARDC,[70] the problem runs deeper than this and is, ultimately, linked to the very dynamics of civil war. As political scientists Koen Vlassenroot and Timothy Raeymaekers have argued, at the heart of the international community's peacebuilding strategy for the DRC lies a basic problem: 'it left out a potential party – the government. By singling out non-state forces as "irregular" groups, it has opened the door to a series of manipulations by Kinshasa's hardliners, who have never abandoned the option of military confrontation.'[71] This is one reason why 'the current strategy of peacebuilding in the DRC leads to the amplification rather than the containment of armed violence'.[72]

The second long-term issue raised by *Operation Artemis* concerns its role as a possible precedent for future operations in which similar 'highly-trained and well-equipped multinational forces' might assist in time-critical stabilisation activities.[73] Even at the time of deployment, some caution about optimism on this score would have been warranted, as the EU flatly turned down UN Peacekeeping Department requests for elements of the IEMF to stay on beyond the mandated period. UN Peacekeeping had made the requests with a view to ensuring a more seamless transition to the larger UN mission, something that might also have served to imbue the new force with trust and local legitimacy. Instead, 'the very strict insistence on the three-month period of deployment signalled clearly to all … the transitory nature of the force'.[74] Since then, EU member states have proved divided and reluctant to take on similar tasks, notwithstanding the fact that 13 EU battle-groups – two of which are on standby 'at all times' and able in theory to deploy 1,500 troops at 15 days' notice – were declared to have reached full operational capability in January 2007.[75] This reluctance became plainly apparent when the humanitarian situation in North Kivu once again deteriorated sharply in the autumn of 2008, placing the UN in the unhappily familiar position of being accused by all sides – local rebel groups and armed factions, the government in Kinshasa, African and Western governments, the international media – of failing to do its job, especially that of protecting civilians. In response to these developments, the UN secretary-general called on the EU to consider providing a 'bridging mission' to the DRC, but France, Germany and, particularly, the UK all firmly ruled out an EU intervention force.[76]

Such reluctance to commit resources and manpower is not unique to the EU, and it needs to be recognised as an important reality against which the declaratory statements by governments expressing 'concern and a determination to act' must be evaluated.

Confronting the gangs and armed groups of Haiti, 2006–07

In February 2004, amid a wave of violence and nearly ten years after his triumphant return from exile, President Jean-Bertrand Aristide was again swept from power in Haiti. His return in 1994 had come on the back of a US-led military intervention authorised by a Security Council resolution that, uniquely, had sanctioned the use of force to restore democracy in the country.[77] Ten years later, however, there was little to show for the intervening decade of UN and Organization of American States-assisted peacebuilding. As a result, the new UN Stabilisation Mission in Haiti (MINUSTAH) established in April 2004 was faced with challenges far more formidable than those of 1994.[78] As if to underscore this reality, MINUSTAH's deployment was followed by a 'massive upsurge in violent crime in the urban centres'.[79] A major part of the new challenge stemmed from the fact that, by the time of Aristide's second departure, Haiti's political economy had become thoroughly criminalised, an unintended consequence of a decade of inter-national peace operations and the near-complete failure to restructure, rebuild and imbue with legitimacy the rule-of-law institutions of the state.[80] Over the next two years, the power of Haiti's gangs went unchecked and violent crime, espe-cially kidnappings, soared as 'a multiplicity of independent and yet interlinked armed groups'[81] became ever more deeply entrenched in the slums and shanty towns of Port-au-Prince, notably Cité Soleil and Martinssant, and other urban centres, such as Gonaïves. By late 2006, Haiti's gangs and armed groups 'were operating with flagrant impunity'.[82] Earlier attempts by MINUSTAH to dislodge the gangs, undertaken in late 2004 and again in July 2005 when it entered Cité Soleil in force, had failed, only serving to embolden the groups further. In late 2006, having first unsuccessfully sought 'dialogue' and voluntary disarmament from the gangs, René Préval, elected president of Haiti earlier in the year, finally sanctioned more decisive use of force in order to restore the authority of the state in gang-controlled areas. That decision proved a turning point.

In a series of operations aimed at clearing out gangs from their strongholds, MINUSTAH, with the support of vetted elements of the Haitian National Police (HNP), went on the offensive. Between late December 2006 and February 2007, 19 'security operations' were launched in Cité Soleil and Martissant alone.[83] In the end, the UN-led operation succeeded in dismantling the 'core of the politicised, criminal networks in Port-au-Prince', giving the country, in the view of the International Crisis Group, an 'historic opportunity to design a democratic future and establish conditions conducive to economic develop-ment'.[84]

While that may be an overly optimistic assessment, there is no doubt that the decision by MINUSTAH to go on the offen-sive played a key role in weakening the grip of a complex and deeply violent gang structure – part criminal, part political – that had by that stage come close to overwhelming the Haitian state completely. The determination to counter armed resis-tance from the gangs with decisive and overwhelming force, something that resulted in minor battles and intense fighting in parts of Port-au-Prince, was critical to the eventual outcome.[85] That determination was aided by and reflected in the military leadership of MINUSTAH, specifically Major-General Carlos Alberto Dos Santos Cruz, a tough Brazilian officer who assumed command of the UN troops in January 2007.[86] A further contrib-uting element, and one critical to the mission's success, was the 'intelligence-driven' nature of operations, in sharp contrast to earlier incursions into the shanty towns and slums, in which UN soldiers and the HNP had been outmanoeuvred by gangs more intimately familiar with Haiti's urban terrain.[87] Collated and processed by MINUSTAH's Joint Mission Analysis Cell

and gathered in part from paid informants and covert surveil-
lance, intelligence enabled more precise targeting of key gang
members, such as the notorious Evens Jeune in Cité Soleil. The
Haitian mission's innovative use of intelligence represented
a noteworthy 'departure from the traditional approach to
"peacekeeping"'.[88] By the end of July 2007, nearly 900 suspects
had been arrested, breaking the hold, at least temporarily, of
the major gangs and bringing about a 'sharp decrease in the
level of violence'.[89]

The long-term effects of confronting the gangs, however, will
depend on whether legitimate state authority can be brought
not only to additional urban areas of Haiti but also to the coun-
tryside and to key ports and border crossings controlled by
organised crime.[90] Beyond that, long-term stability and sustainable peace 'will depend on the ability of Haitian institutions ...
to fill the space vacated by the gangs. In particular, this entails
delivering essential government services, asserting the rule of
law and generating opportunities for employment.'[91] Of critical importance will be an area that has in the past been marked
by conspicuous failure: reform of the police and associated
rule-of-law institutions, both courts and correctional services.
In view of the scale and deep-seated nature of the challenges
facing Haiti – the socio-economic elements of which were
tragically exacerbated by a series of devastating storms and
hurricanes that hit the country in September 2008 – meeting
these objectives was always going to be a formidable challenge. While the action in late 2006–7 reduced levels of violence
significantly, continuing political paralysis has, as in the past,
complicated efforts to exploit the respite. While some progress
was reported in early 2009 on 'political dialogue', the overall
'situation remains very fragile', owing not least (as in Sierra
Leone) to the steadily growing power of drug traffickers and
the corrosive effects of their trade.[92]

The use and utility of force: assessment and wider implications

Operation Palliser, *Operation Artemis* and the military operation to wrest power from armed groups in Haiti in 2006–07 all carry distinctive lessons of their own and care should be taken when drawing wider lessons from such different settings. Nonetheless, five broad conclusions regarding the use of force in peace operations do emerge from the discussion above.

Firstly, the decisive use, or threat of use, of military force may be necessary to stabilise a highly fragile environment and keep a mission from collapse. It is probably the case that 'if MINUSTAH had not been willing and able to confront the gang threat emanating … from Cité Soleil, the mission would likely have been doomed to fail'.[93] Likewise, the deployment of a robust British force to Sierra Leone in May 2000, reinforced by military pressure exerted on the RUF elsewhere in the country, helped to shore up a peacebuilding mission on the verge of collapse. In Bunia, a wider humanitarian catastrophe was prevented and a measure of stability imposed locally by the deployment of the IEMF. Even so, any decision to use force must take account of the possibility of unintended and destabilising consequences elsewhere. The military effectiveness of *Operation Artemis* was highly localised and, as noted, by 'skew[ing] the military balance in Ituri … [it] may indirectly have caused harm elsewhere'.[94]

Secondly, in the short term, the effectiveness of military force in these circumstances is closely connected with the quality of and resources available to the intervening force, specifically in terms of its ability to deploy rapidly, to employ overwhelming force and to exploit its local military superiority and technological advantages. Not least important is the psychological edge and boost to confidence that a highly capable and well-trained force is able to provide. Intelligence in particular is a critical requirement for forces operating in volatile and complex operational environments, and indeed the exploitation of intelligence was central to the outcome of all three of the operations examined, especially in Haiti.[95]

Thirdly, in the longer run, the effectiveness of military force depends crucially on the clarity of overall political objectives, reflected in coordinated and properly resourced follow-up action to consolidate short-term achievements. The comparative success of *Palliser* must be viewed in the light of the UK's decision to follow up military deployments with vigorous diplomatic action, while at the same time making the country a major aid recipient and, above all, committing itself for the long haul to a programme of capacity-building of Sierra Leone's security sector and armed forces.[96] Absent the determination to build on short-term tactical gains in this way, the robust use of force may well end up having destabilising consequences by upsetting local balances of power and drawing outsiders more deeply into local conflicts.

Fourthly, one of the conclusions drawn by Brian Urquhart from events in Sierra Leone was that the 'UN must have highly trained and universally respected rapid reaction force on its own, acting on the directives of the Security Council'.[97] This, however, is not going to happen; indeed, one of the chief lessons to emerge from peace-intervention operations since 2000 is that the kind of robust military force that can make a critical difference at key moments, even if committed only as an 'over-the-horizon' force, will be raised with great difficulty, if at all. As the situation regarding the availability of EU battlegroups makes clear, this is only partly a question of limited resources; it also reflects deeper political divisions and uncertainties among potential troop contributors.

In one sense, the final conclusion merely reinforces all of this. In 1994, Lieutenant-General Rupert Smith argued that the reason why the use of force 'in intervention operations' after the Cold War had often ended 'with disappointing or unlooked-for consequences' was that 'we had been unclear as to what it is we expect the use of force or forces to *achieve* as opposed to *do'*.[98] Smith made this observation before he himself assumed command of UN forces in Bosnia and before many of the operations discussed in this book had been embarked upon. Yet, as all three of the examples given here show, the distinction he drew remains critically important to the question of the use of force both in the early stages of and throughout 'peacebuilding' operations.

Stabilising governance structures and providing basic services

Central government and local governance

While strengthening governance capacity and administrative structures is widely recognised as key to attaining stability and reducing insecurity in post-conflict societies, it has proved one of the most difficult of the challenges facing outsiders in the early phase of interventions. In part this is because the attention of external actors has often been misdirected, with the principal focus being on systems of central government and political life in the capital rather than on local, municipal and regional governance. The suggestion here is not that questions relating to the organisation of central government and the country-wide challenges facing a war-torn society should be set aside lightly or that the tackling of them should be indefinitely postponed; rather it is a question of balance and of recognising that serious attention to local government and local issues is not only important in its own right but may also offer a more promising route to stability in the early post-war phase.

There are three reasons why the focus on central government is problematic and has at times proved destabilising in the early phase of 'post-conflict' operations and, conversely, why attention to the local level is essential.

Firstly, the organisation of central government raises the most politically contentious of issues, with disputes over the format of elections, the formation of political parties and constitutional matters tending to become, at best, a source of paralysis; more often than not, the process deepens societal divisions and generates more conflict. Indeed, where 'state-building' efforts and attempts to end violent conflict have concentrated primarily on working out power arrangements at the centre, through power-sharing mechanisms and accords, the process of arriving at those arrangements has often turned into a 'conflict-producing exercise', with actors treating it as a zero-sum game.[99] In many cases, working out relations between centre and periphery has proved a particularly daunting challenge, usually for deeply rooted historical reasons but also because of the effects that protracted war and violence have had on state–society relations. With respect to Afghanistan, for example, Afghan scholar Amin Saikal has emphasised how the country has long been 'dominated by a web of overlapping micro-societies' and that while

> plans to create a strong centralized state in Afghanistan are intended to overcome divisions between the micro-societies ... they run the risk of merely papering over the political dynamics that these micro-societies represent. The only way to secure a stable political environment is to embrace those dynamics and design political structures around them accordingly.[100]

In the short run, designing such 'political structures', while arguably essential to long-term stability, inevitably becomes an arena of intense political contestation. Added to the difficulties of rebuilding central government and/or imbuing it with wide-spread legitimacy is the reality that the centre, especially in the immediate aftermath of protracted conflict, is often viewed with deep suspicion and distrust outside the capital, which tends to be seen as a place of intrigue and political infighting divorced from the daily challenges of coping and survival.

Secondly, in the short term, the issue of the organisation of central government tends to be of little direct relevance to those whose immediate concerns are with security and the continued supply or reinstatement of essential services, including water, sanitation, food, public health and power. Added to this is the fact that in environments where the provision of services by central authorities has broken down as a result of violence and war, people will often – as the political-economy perspective set out earlier makes clear – have developed 'inventiveness and entrepreneurial skills … at the level of daily life', and services one would 'expect to be under the control of [government are] organised in neighbourhoods, by ad hoc committees or by local business'.[101] This not a universal pattern, and some places where the tendency is especially marked, for example parts of Somalia – war-torn and stateless now for nearly two decades – are thought by some to be unique examples of 'local ingenu-ity in the absence of state control'.[102] Even so, such examples are only particularly striking instances of a well-documented more general phenomenon: war and protracted conflict often encourage a 'radical localisation'[103] of politics and econom-ics, as formal institutions wither and are replaced by informal mechanisms more attuned to local demands for security.

This brings us directly to the third reason why greater atten-tion needs to be given – analytically as well as by practitioners and policymakers engaged in peacebuilding – to local-level developments and realities: the absence of government does not invariably mean the absence of governance.

Writing in 1993, George Kennan lamented his country's recent involvement in Somalia as 'a dreadful error of American policy'.[104] 'The situation we are trying to correct', he wrote with characteristic clarity and apparent authority, 'has its roots in the fact that the people of Somalia are wholly unable to govern themselves and that the entire territory is simply without a government'.[105] Since then, Somalia has indeed remained without an effective central government, earning it the distinction of being the 'longest-running instance of complete state collapse in postcolonial history'.[106] And yet, Kennan was plainly wrong in supposing that Somalis where 'wholly unable to govern themselves'. While the Somali state has collapsed and shows few signs of revival, an informal 'mosaic of local polities and informal social pacts' have evolved in the country that offer 'some level of "governance", if not "government"', especially outside the south-central region.[107] The greatest amount of change in terms of improved governance in Somalia has been at the municipal and neighbourhood levels, though varying degrees of governance have also emerged across wider regions, primarily in the north of the country, in the region of Puntland and, most notably and most impressively, the unrecognised state of Somaliland, where substantial improvements have taken place both in public security and economic recovery since the mid 1990s.[108] These changes, according to Ken Menkhaus, 'reflect what could be described as an "organic", local revival of governance', which does not amount to a central state but which has nonetheless 'provided Somalis with a modicum of rule of law and predictability in a dangerous environment'.[109] Moreover, local governance structures have had the crucial 'advantage of enjoying a high degree of legitimacy and local ownership'.[110]

This latter point is illustrated by the example of the Council of Somali Islamic Courts' brief rule in south-central Somalia in

2006. In early 2006, the Council of Somali Islamic Courts established control in Mogadishu, and for some six months before being ousted by Ethiopian forces it was the 'pre-eminent political and military authority in southern Somalia'.[111] According to long-time observer of the Somali scene Matt Bryden, the Courts succeeded in establishing 'a degree of stability and security across most of southern Somalia not seen since the Siyaad Barre era'; it did so in part because it responded to and satisfied above all local needs and concerns around basic security, something that was reflected by its 'strong popular support base'.[112]

While the experience of Somalia is in some ways unique, it raises a number of questions that are of wider interest, beyond the obvious issue of the need for any outside force to pay 'close attention to the local political culture in any operation'.[113] In Somalia, the state 'had not only failed, it was an exotic import in the first place' and precisely because the state had 'struck very shallow roots ... the legitimacy of the intervention ... had to be established at the local, not at the state, level'.[114] The case of Somalia also raises further questions about supposedly 'ungoverned' societies and spaces: how 'politics operate in the absence of a government; how markets function without legal institutions and currencies; how communities draw on customary forms of identity and organisation to tap markets and weather extraordinary levels of instability'.[115] As these questions have been applied to other cases, similar patterns of adaptation to extreme circumstances are often found to have emerged:

> Communities that have been cut off from an effective state authority – whether out of governmental indifference to marginal frontier territories, or because of protracted warfare, or because of vested local and external interests in perpetuating conditions of state

failure – consistently seek to devise arrangements to provide for themselves the core functions that the missing state is supposed to assume, especially basic security.[116]

To anthropologists who have studied the impact of violence and protracted conflict on local communities, these are not necessarily new findings. As Paul Richards has noted, 'the institutional fabric to keep armed conflict within bounds over the longer term sometimes emerges from below as well as from above', and the contribution of ethnographic and anthropological work on armed conflict may well be to show that the 'interests [of war-affected peoples] might be better served by reform of local government and justice than a reconstruction of the state'.[117]

Even where the collapse of the state is as complete and comprehensive as it was in Iraq in April–May 2003, efforts to restore stability and some degree of order often emerge spontaneously from the bottom up. The challenge faced by an outside force in such circumstances lies in working with and not against the grain of local developments that favour stability, though doing so without rewarding intimidation and violence. As Hilary Synnott writes of his time in Iraq, 'when local government institutions were not able to develop, governance itself became a battleground and people sought to gain the spoils of power by intimidation'.[118] Governance at the local level in Iraq was fatally neglected in the early phase of the occupation when, arguably, this was one of the few ways of halting the descent into violence once the existing administrative structures had collapsed.[119] As journalist and author George Packer highlights, the slowness of the Coalition Provisional Authority (CPA) in spelling 'out the authority of local councils ... along with the two-and-half-month stoppage of the military's emergency funds, left the councils and the soldiers working with them in a limbo, bringing reconstruction to a near standstill, and preventing local government from developing into a power centre that could compete with the militias and insurgents for popular support'.[120] These lessons about the importance of paying attention to local governance stand in parallel to the sobering conclusion drawn from Somalia and the myriad attempts to form central government there since the early 1990s that, conversely, 'state-building and peacebuilding can work against each other in the short to medium term'.[121]

Writing on the DRC, Zoë Marriage echoes the findings from Somalia and Iraq, similarly highlighting the importance of outsiders lending their support to 'local-level developments that foster security' throughout the country. In doing so, she introduces a further lesson: that such engagement would require (of MONUC in this case) a more 'sophisticated understanding of how informal networks operate and the role of history, identity and religion in establishing codes of practice and hierarchies of priorities'.[122] Establishing such an understanding, let alone translating it into effective policy on the ground, is of course a great deal easier said than done, and this discussion should not be seen as an attempt to glamorise or portray all initiatives and signs of ingenuity that emerge at the local level as inherently good or positive, or as a kind of true or authentic response of 'civil society' to the predation, manipulation and violence of outsiders or the centre. That would be crude and simplistic. Rather, it is to draw attention to the practical implications of the finding, highlighted in Chapter 1, that societies do not simply 'collapse' into anarchy. Furthermore, the challenge of post-war stabilisation clearly cannot be reduced to a simple question of power-sharing and state-building at the centre *versus* local or bottom-up initiatives: there is a necessary relationship between the two that also needs to be recognised. Doing so requires a further distinction to be made. As Matt Bryden has noted in relation to Somalia:

> It is important to distinguish between 'power-sharing' itself, and definition of the parameters within which power is to be shared: the rules of the game. One common weakness of statebuilding efforts is an emphasis on power-sharing, rather than on the organization of government at all levels. Transitional, power-sharing governments are often reluctant to address these issues since they would often require a dilution of central government and a diminution of central control over systems of patronage and representation. As a result, transitional governments too often fail to reshape government in ways that mitigate the root causes of the crisis. In order for power-sharing to succeed, the principals must understand and agree upon the framework within which power will be shared – however difficult this task may be (this was one of the great failures of the Mbagathi process that led to the formation of Somalia's Transitional Federal Government).[123]

For those deployed in a peacebuilding capacity, important implications flow from the recognition of the importance of local-level developments, including about the need to engage with the informal economy and to recognise the link between formal and informal, licit and illicit, sectors. This can be seen in two sets issues deeply relevant to the struggle for post-war stability: employment and the provision of basic services.

Employment and post-war stabilisation

According to Susan Woodward, 'the most obvious but most neglected lesson' of the experience of implementing peace settlements in the 1990s is the need to tackle 'high levels of unemployment in the first years after war'. This is because 'high levels of unemployment pose a clear threat to peace whether through disillusionment, lack of alternative activity and status, or the continued availability of unemployed for mobilisation by spoilers'.[124] There is much to this argument, as there is to the associated critique of donors – especially the international financial institutions in the 1990s – that charges them with failing to appreciate that in fragile post-war settings the demands of macroeconomic stabilisation will often clash with the more immediate requirements of 'peace' or 'political stabilisation'.[125] Levels of formal unemployment, especially youth unemployment, in post-conflict societies are indeed often very high and can, given the right circumstances and combination of factors, become a source of violence and instability. In Bosnia-Herzegovina, the figure for unemployment stood between 30–40% more than a decade after the signature of the Dayton peace agreement; in 2005, nearly half of Kosovo's workforce was assumed to be 'afflicted by unemployment'.[126] In early 2009, the rate of unemployment nationwide in Iraq was estimated to be somewhere between 23 and 38%.[127]

Even so, care should be taken in assuming that there is a simple causal connection between levels of unemployment on the one hand and violence and instability on the other. Unemployment, like poverty, is not on its own a trigger for violence. If that were the case one would expect to see greater levels of violence than are in fact witnessed in most cases. The concern with unemployment has often been underpinned by an unspoken assumption about the 'effects of idleness' on unemployed populations, an assumption that does not always stand up to closer empirical scrutiny. One of the reasons why official unemployment rates do not tally with expectations of increased associated violence is because high figures such as those cited above rarely take account of informal and 'grey-zone' activity or the entrepreneurial skills and coping mechanisms often displayed by groups of people who are officially not working. As social scientists Morten Bøås and Anne Hatløy found in a detailed survey of ex-combatants in Liberia, their subjects' decisions to take up arms and join militias were more likely to have been motivated by security concerns than by 'idleness and poverty'.[128]

In terms of minimising violence and instability in the immediate post-conflict phase – the focus of attention here – the challenge of post-conflict unemployment is critically linked to that of the disarmament, demobilisation and reintegration of ex-combatants. In brief, where this process has been fragmentary, incomplete and/or poorly conceived, the release from service within a short space of time of large numbers of soldiers – often young men who, while unskilled and ill-prepared for civilian life, may, to borrow Charles Tilly's phrase, be 'specialists' in violence – has unquestionably contributed to dramatic rises in levels of political and criminal violence. As the examples of El Salvador in 1993 and, even more strikingly, Iraq in 2003–4 illustrate, poorly sequenced and rapid demobilisation can be catastrophic for immediate post-war stability.[129] In the latter case, not only was nearly 80% of a 'sample adult population' not in full-time employment in late 2004, but the 'de-Ba'athification' programme ordered by the Coalition Provisional Authority in May 2003 in addition to the disbanding of the army had the immediate effect of removing the top layers of management from the economy.[130] It is the combination of mass and speed of demobilisation in post-conflict settings that has proved so destabilising: too often the ability of local societies and economies to absorb surplus soldiers has simply been overwhelmed by the speed with which large bodies of men have been released from military control and discipline. At the same time, the consequences of ill-handled demobilisations have undermined the legitimacy of outsiders in the eyes of large segments of local populations. As scholars Eric Herring and Glen Rangwala have observed of Iraq, the 'CPA began its rule of Iraq with a programme to dismantle organisations that were also some of Iraq's biggest employers prior to the invasion, and its reputation suffered accordingly'.[131] Again, while Iraq is an extreme case, it points to some general lessons. Any approaches taken to tackling issues of employment and unemployment in the immediate post-conflict phase must proceed from an appreciation of the absorptive capacity of society and local economies and the wider political impact of measures undertaken, not from technical or 'templated solutions'. That lesson also applies to the challenge of restoring and providing basic services to war-weary and vulnerable populations.

Providing basic services

For populations emerging from protracted armed conflict, the first signs of a 'peace dividend', of a visible transformation wrought by the end of war, are improvements in basic, often life-sustaining, services: water, food, sanitation, electricity and public health. Progress in this area, along with the greater sense of security with which any such progress is inextricably linked, is the factor that most directly affects the legitimacy of both outsiders and nascent structures of governance in the early, critical phase of post-conflict operations. This was evident in three otherwise sharply differing cases and circumstances: Haiti in 1994, East Timor in 1999 and Iraq in 2003.

In Haiti, the departure of Raoul Cédras' military junta and the return of Jean-Bertrand Aristide in 1994 raised, as the UN secretary-general observed at the time, 'very high expectations of jobs, education and a better life for all'.[132] Noting that the new government 'could not be expected to meet these expectations less than two months after its formation', Boutros Boutros-

Ghali added that 'the traditionally patient Haitian people' were nonetheless 'starting to complain about high prices and unemployment'.[133] Directly and immediately relevant to levels of violence and stability in the country was the issue of the restoration of basic services:

> The availability of electricity is essential to the resump-
> tion of economic activity, including assembly and light
> manufacturing industry. It has a significant impact
> not only on the mood of the population but also on its
> safety, as a direct correlation has been shown to exist
> between blackouts and crimes.[134]

Similarly, by late 1999, only a few months after the referendum on independence from Indonesia and its bloody and violent aftermath, East Timorese were expressing their anger at the UN presence for failing to bring about rapid improvement in the daily lives of ordinary citizens.[135] In Iraq, George Packer remarks how soldiers on the ground soon discovered that providing the 'basics of life' was key to stability locally and that failure to deliver crucially affected the 'mood of the people'.[136] As one of Packer's interviewees realised, 'sewage [was] the front line of nation-building'.[137] In the cases of both East Timor and Iraq, levels of destruction and damage to economic infra-structure from recent violence were very high, in the former instance because of the destruction inflicted by pro-Indonesian militias, and in the latter as a consequence of three weeks of organised and unhindered looting. In both cases the problem was compounded by the exodus of professional expertise from the country, a feature of many post-conflict settings. The need to restore basic services was therefore acute, quickly becoming as important an issue in the eyes of locals as the acquisition of newly won rights and freedoms. Even in cases where the needs of recovery are less immediately urgent, the absence of visible improvements in the short run has proved a key factor in deflating the euphoria and expectations that accompany the outbreak of peace. The fact that such expectations are often profoundly unrealistic makes 'expectation management' a necessary task for outsiders.[138]

While the importance of managing expectations and providing basic services in the early post-conflict phase is frequently recognised by donors and peacebuilders – as evidenced in part by the growing emphasis on and interest in so-called 'quick-impact' projects – closing the gap between expectations and delivery has proved difficult. This is not just due to the unrealistic nature of the expectations of local populations. Nor is it simply a matter of throwing money and resources at the problem. In Iraq, some $50 billion has been appropriated by US Congress for relief and reconstruction since 2003, and yet Iraq's electricity sector remains severely underdeveloped. When the power grid crashed in Baghdad in 2003, it took other infrastructure systems with it, including potable water, sewage systems and hospital services.[139] Six years on, electricity generation, along with other sectors – notably water and health – has barely recovered to pre-war levels.[140] In Haiti, 'there is today virtually no legacy… of the roughly US$2 billion spent by the international community' between Aristide's return in 1994 and 1998.[141]

The reasons why closing the gap between expectations and delivery has proved difficult are discussed in greater detail below (one important one is the lack of strategic coordination among donor countries, the military and NGOs). Two final and related factors, however, deserve special mention here.

Firstly, peacebuilding activities and interventions have been poorly served by an exaggerated focus on measuring progress in terms of formal quantitative indicators rather than 'outcome indicators'.[142] This, again, was especially pronounced in Iraq, and its damaging consequences have now been acknowledged by US authorities, at least in their 'lessons learned' exercises.[143] With regard to the health sector, for example, senior medical officer with USAID Frederick Burkle has remarked on how the US 'emphasised reconstruction of clinics and hospitals ... rather than what these structures were able to do'.[144] A similar problem was identified by Hilary Synnott, who lamented that US

> briefings were all about 'metrics', which seemed to reflect a peculiarly American fixation with quantifying results in terms of, for instance, the number of schools refurbished, kilometres of roads resurfaced, pipelines repaired and the like. These were figures which our governments liked to publicise. But they conveyed nothing of the reality.[145]

Secondly, while what economists refer to as the 'absorption capacity' of war-ravaged economies is typically low, the informal coping mechanisms and forms of adaptation to the stresses of conflict that will have emerged in the course of war are nevertheless often more likely in the *short run* to deliver basic services effectively than are complex programmes and reconstruction schemes brought in from outside. A UN Development Programme survey of the challenges of post-conflict recovery has recently emphasised the fact that 'wars do not destroy economic life altogether' and that 'war economies' in particular 'reshape, but do not eliminate, patterns of accumulation, exchange and distribution'.[146] In the specific case of health-service delivery in post-conflict settings, outsiders or 'newcomers' to a conflict zone, one study found, 'are often unaware of promising initiatives developed at the local level in response to the disruption wrought by war'.[147] This finding echoes a recurring theme of this book.

CHAPTER THREE

Organisational and Policy Responses to the Peacebuilding Challenge:
The Case of the UN and its Peacebuilding Commission

The dramatic increase in peacebuilding activity since the early 1990s and, in particular, the unprecedented range and ambitious nature of the tasks now subsumed under the rubric of peacebuilding, have placed major demands – of a conceptual as well as a more practical kind – on donor countries and international organisations. The ways in which governments and organisations have responded to the challenges that have emerged are worth examining in some detail. The discussion here is framed around a detailed assessment of the evolution and functioning of the UN's Peacebuilding Commission (PBC) and its associated peacebuilding 'architecture'. The reason for this choice of focus is threefold.

Firstly, the UN remains, for better or worse, a dominant actor in the peacebuilding field and the PBC represents a concrete and considered move to identify policy challenges and improve the UN's performance after some 20 years of 'post-conflict' peacebuilding experience. Whether it is mounting operations under its own flag, acting jointly with others or merely conferring legitimacy on the actions of states and regional organisations, the UN is likely to remain a key player in the field for the foreseeable future.

Secondly, the challenges that the PBC has been designed to address – the need for improved analysis and understanding of peacebuilding environments, for better coordination among multiple actors, greater efficiency in the delivery and marshalling of financial and other resources, and greater sensitivity and responsiveness to local needs, including those of civil society – raise broader issues of policy in relation to peacebuilding, issues that also confront individual governments and regional organisations.

Thirdly, fashioning policy and creating organisational structures to support peacebuilding is not simply a technocratic exercise. Actual outcomes are inescapably marked by intramural and international politics, that is, by tensions and competition over resources, priorities and policies among both states and international bureaucracies. The interests of those states and, in particular, the views they hold about the appropriate role of outsiders – whether the UN or individual states – in building 'peace' within states often differ sharply. The history of the PBC brings out this reality very clearly. Thus, the commission's evolution from the conceptual drawing-board to its current incarnation offers important clues about the political and practical obstacles that lie in the way of a more effective and coordinated international approach to peacebuilding. As is so often the case, the UN here reflects deeper fault lines within the international system. These, more than any other set of factors, are likely to determine whether, and in what form, international peacebuilding will remain the kind of growth industry it has been for much of the post-Cold War era.

The establishment of the UN Peacebuilding Commission

In a stirring and memorable address to the General Assembly in September 2003, Secretary-General Kofi Annan declared that the UN had reached a 'fork in the road' and that now was the moment to consider radical reform of the world body.[1] The speech marked the beginning of a reform drive that would culminate two years later in the largest-ever gathering of heads of state and government in New York, the 'World Summit' of 2005. Annan saw his call for reform as a necessary response to the deep tensions running through the UN membership that the American-led invasion of Iraq in 2003 had sharply exposed and exacerbated. Those very tensions, however, were always going to frustrate and complicate the reform drive itself, especially one as wide-ranging, ambitious and thorough as that envisaged by Annan. In particular, given the climate of open mistrust and ill-concealed bitterness that had come to characterise politics at the UN in the aftermath of the US-led invasion of Iraq, Annan's insistence on the substantive reform of intergovernmental bodies, notably the Security Council, was bound to intensify political divisions among member states. And indeed, as world leaders prepared to depart New York after the summit in September 2005, a sense of relief rather than achievement was palpable among UN officials. The Summit had come perilously close to being a grand failure, with agreement on a 'Final Outcome Document' reached only at the very last minute.[2] The divisions exposed during the summit and its preparations have, if anything, deepened since 2005, notwithstanding the election of a new secretary-general in 2006 and a new US president in 2008, and they now provide an important and inescapable contextual backdrop to any assessment of the future of international peacebuilding.

One aspect of the near-failure of the World Summit was that the meeting left a number of concrete proposals and ideas presented by Annan in advance of the gathering in a form that was heavily modified, lacking in detail and with most of the thornier issues they necessarily raised held over for 'subsequent negotiations' by member states. One of these was the proposal to create a Peacebuilding Commission and an associated Peacebuilding Support Office. Originally proposed by the High-Level Panel on Threats, Challenges and Change (HLP) set up in the wake of Annan's 'fork-in-the-road' speech, the idea of a PBC, unlike some, survived the reform process, albeit far from unscathed.[3] Established as an 'intergovernmental advisory body' by, uniquely, concurrent resolutions of the Security Council and the General Assembly in December 2005, the PBC was formally inaugurated in June 2006 and presented its first annual report in July 2007.[4] The commission meets in two major configurations: the Organisational Committee, a kind of steering committee with representation from 31 member states; and committees devoted to particular countries. There is also a 'Working Group on Lessons Learned'. Four country-specific committees – for Sierra Leone, Burundi, Guinea–Bissau and the Central African Republic (CAR) – have thus far been created. The work of the PBC is supported, as originally envisaged, by a Peacebuilding Support Office (PBSO) within the UN Secretariat, whose tasks are to advise the secretary-general on 'effective strategies of peacebuilding' and to 'oversee the operation of the Peacebuilding Fund'.[5] That fund – a multi-donor standing trust fund to support peacebuilding activities in their early critical stages – was set up in October 2006, becoming the third pillar of the UN's new 'peacebuilding architecture'.

The establishment of the PBC has attracted much attention and received strong support – albeit almost invariably expressed in broad and general terms – from the UN membership as a whole. This is not merely because it is one of the few concrete achievements to have emerged from Kofi Annan's ambitious reform drive. It was also generally accepted that the challenge it was designed to meet was real and urgent: to provide a 'dedicated institutional mechanism to address the special needs of countries emerging from conflict towards recovery, reintegration and reconstruction and to assist them in laying the foundation for sustainable development'.[6] Beyond this, however, member states have remained deeply divided about the precise role of the PBC – what it will do and how it will function. These divisions account for the large amount of time spent since the commission's creation on the discussion of 'organizational, procedural and methodological' issues.[7] As originally conceived by the HLP, the PBC was intended to be a body with real decision-making powers, institutionally aligned to the Security Council and with the ability, in theory at least, to provide 'proactive assistance' to countries 'under stress' or at risk from 'state collapse'.[8] In its final incarnation in the Outcome Document of the World Summit, it is an 'advisory subsidiary organ' of both the General Assembly and the Security Council.[9] It has no operational capacity of its own and the rules and arrangements governing its role that were formulated in the wake of the summit – including rules about procedures, working methods and reporting lines to intergovernmental organs – are, insofar as they have been clarified, indelibly marked by the political tensions and fault lines of the organisation as a whole.

Despite this, the creation of the PBC, the PBSO and the Peacebuilding Fund is not without significance for two reasons. Firstly, the original rationale for setting up the PBC reflects issues of concern to all external actors engaged in peacebuilding, whether the UN itself, regional organisations or individual member states. Moreover, the activities of the PBC since 2006 – especially in its country-specific configurations – highlight enduring and fundamental peacebuilding challenges. Secondly, the move from what on paper was a robust and focused body to something altogether more woolly and vague tells us a great deal about the obstacles inherent in UN reform generally, about the highly charged political atmosphere in which reform has been undertaken and, by extension, about the real prospects for a more systematic and coordinated approach to international peacebuilding. It is easy enough to create a perfect theoretical institutional structure. The evolution and current workings of the PBC bring out the importance of the political and bureaucratic forces that have shaped the actual outcome of an initiative designed, quite justifiably, to improve on a record of international 'peacebuilding' performance that has, too often, been blighted by a lack of overall strategic direction, the absence of coordination among a wide range of actors and a lack of funds at critical moments and stages of an operation.

Origins and rationale

As detailed above, the history of UN operational activity since the early 1990s is distinguished by a dramatic expansion of the organisation's role in efforts to consolidate peace within societies affected by war and violent conflict. The level and intensity of UN involvement has of course varied greatly. Even so, with the exception of a period of retrenchment between 1996 and 1999 following the traumatic experience of UN-mandated forces in Bosnia and Rwanda, the general trend has been one of growth in the size of missions and increased complexity of their mandates. By mid 2009, the number of police, soldiers and military observers deployed on UN missions worldwide had risen to well over 90,000.[10] With civilian and local staff added to that figure, the total number of personnel serving under UN auspices is close to 115,000. At the same time, the UN peacekeeping budget for 2009–10 has been tentatively set at $8.2 billion, an increase of $2.8bn over the budget for 2007–08. Crucially, with the exception of the UN Mission for the Referendum in Western Sahara (MINURSO), all of the 11 ongoing UN field operations launched after 1990 have had a 'peacebuilding' dimension to their mandates, that is to say, they have incorporated one or more of the 'post-conflict' activities subsumed under the heading of 'peacebuilding' by the 2000 Brahimi Panel on UN Peace Operations. As identified by the panel, these activities include but are 'not limited to reintegrating former combatants into civilian society, strengthening the rule of law; improving respect for human rights through the monitoring, education and investigation of past and existing abuses; providing technical assistance for democratic development … ; and promoting conflict resolution and reconciliation techniques'.[11]

The sheer growth and scope of UN involvement in the peacebuilding field, then, provided an important stimulus for the creation of the Peacebuilding Commission. This growing involvement has also highlighted certain recurring weaknesses and deficiencies in the UN's post-conflict recovery efforts. As originally conceived, the PBC may be viewed as an attempt to address four overlapping needs made manifest by more than two decades of UN peacebuilding activity:

- The need for international action to be taken early, ideally in a preventative fashion, when faced with weak, vulnerable and fragile states on the verge of lapsing or, more likely, relapsing into violent conflict;
- The need for improved strategic direction and coordination of international peacebuilding efforts, including better integration and coherence of effort within the extended family of UN bodies, including the international financial institutions;
- The need to find more effective ways of involving civil-society actors in the rebuilding of war-torn societies;
- The need for prompt and adequate funding of peacebuilding activities, especially in their early, time-dependent and critical recovery phase.

Because these needs are all in important respects also generic peacebuilding challenges, reflecting the experiences of regional organisations and individual donor countries as well as the UN, they merit more detailed discussion.

Early engagement and prevention
The case for international involvement at an early stage in a conflict cycle – to prevent a situation from deteriorating further but also in order to improve the prospects for effective action to be taken at all – is, certainly in the abstract, compelling, and a large body of advocacy-cum-policy-oriented literature is now devoted to the subject of conflict prevention.[12] Individual governments, especially those that are strongly supportive of the UN and its 'post-conflict' activities – notably the Nordic countries, Canada and Germany – have also repeatedly stressed the need for preventive and more proactive engagement with conflict-strewn and fragile societies, especially those emerging from war.[13] Although, for reasons discussed earlier, the notion of state 'failure' or 'collapse' as it features in much of the literature on state-building is analytically problematic, the challenge of extreme state weakness compounded by conditions of 'neither war nor peace' remains a real one. It explains why giving the PBC a capacity to address this highly sensitive and politically delicate issue was at the heart of the HLP's original proposal. Among the 'core functions' of the body that the proposal envisaged was the task of identifying 'countries which are under stress and risk sliding towards State collapse' and organising 'proactive assistance in preventing that process from developing further'.[14] The importance attached to this function was further reflected in the suggestion that the Peacebuilding Support Office within the Secretariat should 'submit twice-yearly early-warning analyses to the Peacebuilding Commission to help it in organizing its work'.[15]

Strategic direction and coordination

Strategy is fundamentally concerned with the efficient use of available means and resources in support of a particular end. As an actor in the field of peacebuilding – in many cases the key actor – the UN has proved notoriously poor at thinking and behaving in strategic terms.[16] In part, the problem is a practical one. The UN 'system' is heavily and famously decentralised, with sprawling fiefdoms and vested bureaucratic interests that make any attempt to pull in the same direction, even if there is agreement on the direction in which to pull, exceedingly difficult. The secretary-general, in theory at the apex of the system, has in reality never been more than a *primus inter pares*, with convening powers and a certain clout that goes with the office, but little else. The scale of the undertaking represented by many large-scale peacebuilding operations has merely magnified an existing problem within what has long been a 'highly stove-piped organisation'.[17] As yet another High-Level Panel – this time on UN 'system-wide coherence' – candidly concluded in its final report of November 2006, the 'UN has become fragmented and weak ... [with] a proliferation of agencies, mandates and offices creating duplication and dulling the focus on outcomes, with moribund entities never discontinued'.[18] It further noted that 'operational incoherence between UN funds, programmes and agencies is most evident' at the country level.[19] Of particular concern has long been the need to bring on board the Bretton Woods institutions, which since the mid 1990s have become increasingly involved in 'post-conflict' activities but have continued to maintain an ambiguous and ill-defined relationship with the core parts of the UN system.

But the problem of the strategic direction of UN peacebuilding efforts, or rather the lack thereof, has also been a *conceptual* one. As noted at the outset, the way in which the term 'peacebuilding' itself has been defined and used within the UN

– covering everything from 'political, legal, institutional, military, humanitarian, human-rights-related [to] environmental, economic and social, cultural or demographic' challenges[20] – offers no guidance or mechanism for setting strategic priorities. It was hoped that the PBC might, given proper clout and authority, fill a 'key institutional gap' here and, by differentiating between multiple aims, begin the process of placing them in a strategic relationship with one another.

The difficulties encountered in ensuring strategic direction and coordination of peacebuilding efforts are not confined to the UN or multilateral bodies, though for obvious reasons the range of competing interests in such organisations is greater than at the national level.[21] Indeed, while Western governments have over the past decade invested much effort and money in reorganising the machinery of government to improve the effectiveness of their engagements in post-conflict settings, achieving unity of effort and internal agreement on strategic priorities has proved hard. This has often been a direct result of a basic 'lack of underlying consensus among departments on national objectives'.[22] The case of the UK, a country that according to one review has been 'at the forefront of conceiving and adopting integrated policy responses to weak and failing states',[23] offers a good illustration of the difficulties faced by many countries in this area.

Since 1997, when the incoming Labour government of Tony Blair committed itself publicly to promoting 'joined-up-government', the UK has sought to break down a deeply entrenched and historically 'strong sense of vertically organised separation' within government, encouraging instead horizontal integration and issue-driven approaches to policymaking among departments.[24] This struggle against 'departmentalism' – making use of new cross-departmental agencies, integrated funding mechanisms or 'pools' and, generally, encouraging the ethos of a 'comprehensive approach' to post-conflict challenges – has led to major organisational changes to the way in which the UK addresses post-conflict countries and scenarios.[25] Specifically, the creation of the Post-Conflict Reconstruction Unit in 2004 (renamed the Stabilisation Unit in 2007) 'significantly enhanc[ed] Whitehall's capacity for horizontal coordination'.[26] However, as Stuart Gordon has observed, the unit's 'authority within Whitehall was severely limited from the outset'.[27] These limitations have been most evident in relation to individual conflicts, notably Afghanistan and Iraq, which have revealed how difficult it is to set '"strategic" priorities rather than simply reconciling departmental interests'.[28] Efforts to operationalise the 'comprehensive approach' in the process of developing British policy towards Afghanistan testified 'to the difficulties in developing even a common sense of "mission" that is able to bind the activities of departments'.[29] The particular difficulty for the Stabilisation Unit has been that it is 'restricted to working only when tasked by a management board comprising its three parent departments [the Ministry of Defence, the Foreign and Commonwealth Office and the Department for International Development] and, lacking its own cabinet minister, it has only a weak capacity to "direct"'.[30] According to one source, this is one reason why there was in effect no Reconstruction Unit involvement – and, more generally, no meaningful 'joined-up government' discussions – in advance of the Afghanistan deployment in 2005.[31]

The difficulties experienced by the UK in this area have, to a greater or lesser degree, been experienced by all major donor countries over the past two decades, and the tri-departmental tension between defence, foreign and development ministries will be familiar to most countries engaged in the peacebuilding field.[32] As this example of the difficulties of developing a common strategy suggests, even within a donor government, the challenge of ensuring strategic coherence is rarely amenable to a bureaucratic fix. The conclusion reached by political scientists Stewart Patrick and Kaysie Brown in relation to the UK resonates with other comparable countries, regional organisations and the UN: 'improved communication, common resource pools, and policy coordination mechanisms can improve policy response but are no substitute for a clear, agreed upon strategic framework reflecting common priorities'.[33] It is worth noting that the EU arguably has a more dysfunctional institutional structure in this area than the UN. At its heart is the tension between the European Council and the European Commission, both of which have responsibilities in 'crisis management and stability operations' but which also both make use of their 'own planning, assessment and execution capabilities, relying on ad hoc coordination at the working level for any attempt at policy coherence'.[34]

Engaging civil society

'Civil-society organisations' and 'civil-society actors' are easily abused terms. Too often there has been a tendency to simplistically view such groups, usually in contradistinction to state structures or commercial interests, as inherently 'good', as somehow outside and untainted by politics, and with a role to play in post-conflict settings that is, almost by definition, constructive and helpful. This view fails to take account of the range and diversity of civil-society actors, which come in many shapes and sizes and can quite plainly make both positive and harmful contributions to peacebuilding efforts on the ground.[35] Nor is there any reason to suppose that the radicalisation of viewpoints and the rupture of societal bonds associated with war and violence, both consequences of conflict that peacebuilding interventions are partly intended to tackle, should not also affect civil-society groups. That said, it is unquestionably the case that the 'state–society relationship' has been neglected 'as the central dynamic in the process of both rebuilding a state apparatus and recreating a "new" society out of the ashes of conflict'.[36] As the political-economy perspective set out above makes clear, the state–society relationship and, specifically, the ways in which that relationship will have been moulded and transformed by war, instability and protracted violence, is central to an understanding of the local dynamics of conflict and the 'social orders' that will have emerged and crystallised during the course of war.

More straightforwardly, peacebuilding activities by their very nature involve a large number of actors outside the formal machinery of governments, whether NGOs or other civil-society representatives, whose activities require harnessing and coordination. Both these factors – the importance of gaining a better understanding of 'state–society' relations, and the need to coordinate actions with non-governmental players – place a premium on engagement, and the creation of mechanisms to foster such engagement, with local civil-society actors.

Predictability of funding and speed of disbursement
An issue that has long bedevilled UN field operations – both those of a traditional peacekeeping kind and the more complex missions undertaken by the organisation since the success of the UN operation in Namibia in 1989–90 – has been the lack of available funds and discretionary funding authority at the field level in the early and critical start-up phase of a mission.[37] A large part of the problem has been the UN's Byzantine procurement system, whose rules and regulations are only intelligible once their deep roots in political power struggles between member states are taken into account, something which also explains why, over the years, they have proved near-impervious to reform.

Similarly, UN budget practices have long been deeply politicised. Perhaps the most obvious example of this can be seen in the long-standing habit of excessive micro-management of the Secretariat's budget by the Administrative and Budgetary Committee of the General Assembly (Fifth Committee) and, specifically, the Advisory Committee on Administrative and Budgetary Questions (ACABQ).[38] This habit is closely connected to the fact that control of the purse strings is one of the few areas where the organisation's wider membership retains real power and influence, at least of a blocking or delaying kind, resulting in a ACABQ that has, 'like the 5th Committee', 'in practice ... tended to be political rather than technical'.[39]

In the meantime, the problems relating to the predictability and rate of disbursement of funds for UN operations have remained. Funding for UN peacebuilding, as opposed to traditional peacekeeping or more conventional development activities, has faced the additional problem of falling into a 'grey area', with funding gaps often arising in areas considered, for obvious reasons, politically sensitive by donor countries, notably the reform of the military and the wider security sector of a member state.[40] To address this deficiency, the HLP proposed a standing fund for peacebuilding of at least $250 million to allow greater predictability, more rapid disbursement and flexibility in the use of funds in the early phase of a mission.[41] In addition to addressing emergency needs that could not await the outcome of the slow, complex and heavily politicised process of budgetary approval in New York, the fund was also 'meant to catalyse and encourage longer term engagement' by other agencies and donors.[42]

A death by many cuts: the politics of peacebuilding

In order for the UN to begin to address these overlapping needs effectively, the HLP originally envisaged the creation of the PBC as a subsidiary organ of the Security Council. This was partly because of the political significance that such a direct link signalled, but also because of the Council's greater authority and comparative effectiveness as an intergovernmental organ. The perceived need for peacekeeping *and* peacebuilding operations, which in practice always overlap as activities in the field, to be brought together on the Council's agenda was a further reason for locating the PBC directly under the Council.[43] It was also envisaged that the PBC would be 'reasonably small', with its standing body, the Organisational Committee, comprising no more than 12 to 15 member states.[44] Its precise powers, in terms of decision-making and executive functions, were not laid down by the HLP, though the rationale and logic of the panel's thinking pointed plainly to something more than just a grand forum for consultation.

The process whereby these original ideas for a PBC were transformed into present arrangements may be seen as involving three phases. In the course of that process the assertion of competing political and bureaucratic interests – among member states but also within the UN system itself – gradually combined to denude the boldness of the initial conception. The first phase ran from the presentation of the initial proposal through to the announcement by the secretary-general of his own reform package – 'In Larger Freedom' – in late March 2005.[45] The second phase covered the period between Annan's presentation and the World Summit in September 2005 when the decision to create the PBC was formally made.[46] The final stage covers the period since then, a period which, in theory at any rate, should have been devoted to fleshing out and giving some real substance to the 'idea' of the PBC.[47]

From the report of the High-Level Panel to 'In Larger Freedom'
'In Larger Freedom', presented by Kofi Annan to the General Assembly in March 2005, endorsed the HLP's appeal for a body that would fill a 'gaping hole in the UN's institu-

tional machinery' and called on member states to 'create an intergovernmental Peacebuilding Commission, as well as a Peacebuilding Support Office'.[48] It emphatically ruled out, however, one of the key functions envisaged for the PBC by the HLP: an early-warning and monitoring role in relation to countries that are 'under stress and risk sliding towards State collapse'.[49] That aspect of the original proposal was always likely to provoke a strong negative reaction from developing countries, voicing their collective opinion on UN reform through the platform of the Non-Aligned Movement (NAM) and the Group of 77 (G-77), bodies that have largely outlived their original purposes but which have, especially in recent years, proved effective as intergovernmental caucus groups for articulating the views of the 'global South' within UN forums and conference settings. What explains the negative reaction? In early 2005, at one of many academic gatherings convened to discuss the HLP and its recommendations, former Indian Foreign Minister Muchkund Dubey spoke specifically to the subject of the panel's proposal for a PBC. If implemented, he maintained, its establishment would have:

> the effect of institutionalising continuing interventions in the domestic affairs of the developing-country members of the UN. The mandate of identifying countries that are under stress and risk sliding towards state collapse is a very wide one, under which any developing member state can be kept under surveillance. The identification of such states will be highly subjective and political factors, particularly the strategic and other interests of major powers, would play a decisive role. This recommendation amounts to creating a new trusteeship system in the UN – not to assist the emergence of colonial countries into independence, as

was the mandate of the Trusteeship Council, but as a means to bring independent sovereign states from the developing world under a new form of colonization.[50]

While such views are difficult to reconcile with the reason why the HLP proposed the PBC – that is, an entirely justifiable concern with improving the UN's operational effectiveness in the field of peacebuilding – it would be wrong to dismiss them as merely paranoid. Although reservations about the proposals for the PBC were usually expressed in far more diplomatic terms than those of Dubey's critique, it quickly became clear that developing countries would be deeply unhappy with a PBC active in anything other than a 'post-conflict' capacity, and were especially concerned about the possibility of a body 'empowered to monitor and pay close attention to countries at risk'.[51] The reason for this was twofold.

Firstly, developing countries have, through the G-77 and NAM, all along insisted that the PBC should focus on 'development' issues in countries emerging from conflict.[52] In its formal statement responding to the first annual report of the PBC, the NAM 'emphasize[d] that the development aspects of any strategy geared towards extricating countries emerging from conflict cannot be over-emphasized'.[53] The practical implications of this insistence have, however, never been spelled out in any detail, beyond a generally expressed desire to establish a 'close link' between the PBC and the UN's Economic and Social Council (ECOSOC), however dysfunctional and lacking in operational capacity that body has long proved itself to be. The focus on development here needs to be seen, therefore, as part of a more general sense among developing nations that 'the Report [of the HLP as a whole] does not adequately address many issues of concern to the South'.[54]

Secondly, and more fundamentally, as Dubey's comments make very clear, it was feared that a monitoring and prevention role for the PBC would pose yet another threat to the principle of non-intervention in the internal affairs of member states, a principle already perceived to be under threat from the growing tendency, exemplified above all by NATO's 1999 Kosovo campaign, for Western countries or Western-led coalitions to justify military intervention on humanitarian grounds.[55] To many countries of the 'global South', justification on such grounds amounts to an appropriation of the 'vocabulary of virtue ... in service of power'.[56] The US doctrine of pre-emption promulgated in the aftermath of the attacks of 11 September 2001 and laid out in that country's National Security Strategy of 2002 (and reaffirmed in 2006) further nourished the sense that principles seen as vital to protecting the weaker states from more powerful ones were under siege. Muchkund Dubey's attempt to encapsulate these concerns in his comments on the HLP resulted in a statement that was plainly crude, simplistic and unqualified, and developing countries are themselves far from immune from the practice of cloaking interests and power-political considerations in the language of virtue and principle. Even so, it is clear that the notion of an early warning and monitoring role, leading to preventive action, only reinforced a long-standing and strongly held conviction among the G-77 that Western powers and the US in particular, if they did not bypass multilateral mechanisms and institutions altogether, were actively seeking to mould them to serve the 'strategic and other interests of major powers'.[57] That conviction has only intensified since 2005, with potentially important implications for the future of international peacebuilding activity.

The political context sketched above also helps to explain another source of concern to the G-77 that Kofi Annan's 'In Larger Freedom' sought to address: the relationship between the proposed peacebuilding commission and the Security Council. Whereas the HLP envisaged the PBC as a subsidiary organ under the Council, 'In Larger Freedom' recognised more clearly the need, for reasons of legitimacy and probably also in order to pre-empt likely objections, to involve other intergovernmental bodies, notably ECOSOC. Still, the secretary-general accepted, rightly of course, that muddled reporting lines and unclear institutional status would be likely to affect the efficiency of any proposed body. Accordingly, he suggested that the PBC 'would best combine efficiency with legitimacy if it were to report to the Security Council and the Economic and Social Council in *sequence*, depending on the phase of the conflict'.[58] 'Simultaneous reporting lines', Annan added, should be avoided 'because they will create duplication and confusion'.[59] In spite of the secretary-general's modifications, a number of countries have continued to express concerns, present from the start, about the commission being too closely tied to the Security Council.[60] Given the political divisions and bitterness that have engulfed the UN since the US-led invasion of Iraq, those concerns were only reinforced by the US expression of a preference for the PBC to be a subsidiary organ of the Council, for it only to 'take its direction from that body', and for its work to be limited to 'post-conflict stabilization and reconstruction, not development'.[61]

Beyond these concessions to political realities, the most notable of which was the ruling out of prevention as a statutory role for the PBC, 'In Larger Freedom' did not go into further detail about the planned commission, promising instead a 'more fully developed proposal' in advance of the summit later in the year.

The 2005 World Summit and after
This, however, did not happen. At the summit in September 2005, member states agreed in their Outcome Document to

establish the commission as an 'inter-governmental advisory body'. But, apart from inserting the word 'advisory', thereby signalling the body's non-operational role, and providing some more detail on its broad remit and constituent parts, key issues were left for later. These included: the precise role and institutional location of the PBC within the UN system; its size, composition and the internal relationship between the commission's standing body and its country-specific configurations; and its reporting lines and relationship with the PBSO. Indeed, the only other significant addition on the subject of the PBC's modus operandi to be found in the Outcome Document was the document's clear statement that 'the Commission should act in all matters on the basis of consensus of its members'; potentially, at least, a recipe for paralysis.[62]

At one level, the failure to reach detailed agreement on these issues is, of course, hardly unexpected. Viewed as a whole, the period from late 2004 through to the September 2005 summit corresponds closely with what long-time observer of the UN Edward Luck has identified as a familiar 'cycle of UN reform'.[63] It is a cycle that nearly always begins with a 'demand for sweeping renovations' and ends with more limited reform that governments and UN officials then find 'reasons to paint ... in glowing colours', all the while issuing new 'declarations about unfinished work and renewed dedication'.[64] An intermediate stage in this cycle – in this case represented by the modifications made by Kofi Annan to the original proposal from the HLP – consists of the secretary-general translating 'ideas into digestible policy steps for consideration by the membership'.[65] What accounts for this predictable trajectory is the fact that governments tend only to 'become fully engaged as decision points approach and the implications for their national interests become clear'.[66] As these points approach, different perspectives and conflicts of interest among member states emerge more sharply. These invariably place limits on the scope for substantive agreement and force compromises around what are at best piecemeal though potentially useful changes, and at worst, mere bland and empty statements.

The only way in which the 2004–05 reform drive departed from the cycle sketched out by Luck was, discouragingly, in its final stage, that is, the stage where business resumes as usual and 'culminating events' such as the World Summit of 2005 'provide an impetus for the next round of UN reform', thus marking 'beginnings as much as endings in the ongoing reform process'.[67] This time around, the reform process took place within a particularly inauspicious political setting and by the time of the summit, the UN had, as then-Chef de Cabinet to the Secretary-General Mark Malloch Brown later put it, become 'a political bog. Almost nothing moved.'[68] This state of affairs did not improve after the summit ended:

> As soon as the Presidents were gone, battle was joined again. Impassioned divisions between North and South reopened: the North wanted more on security, including an unambiguous definition of terrorism; the South wanted more on development, choosing to treat the huge aid pledges made at Gleneagles in preparation for the Summit as old news and less important than having a few extra officials to service UN meetings on development. On management reform, even more damagingly, developing countries chose to view a stronger Secretary-General with greater authority but also greater accountability as a plot to increase American and Western control over the organization.[69]

In large part, this development, which has inevitably influenced subsequent efforts to operationalise the PBC and its associated bodies, was a function of the wider political crisis at the UN. More specifically, it was tied to the role played by John Bolton, US permanent representative to the UN in the run-up to the summit, with Bolton's presence in New York symptomatic of an unusually fraught relationship between the George W. Bush administration and the UN.[70] At one point during his tenure, the US permanent representative had to be reined in by his own State Department, and his behaviour in pre-summit negotiations left UN officials uncertain about his deeper purpose, about whether his 'real intent was to reform or wreck the UN'.[71] Bolton's record and known hostility to the UN as an institution, however, was never in doubt, and this, coupled with his links to those parts of the Bush administration that shared this disposition, was bound to fuel distrust and ill-feeling.[72]

At the same time, it needs to be stressed, many developing countries did not, and have not since the summit, shied away from engaging in their own form of hypocrisy and grandstanding, professing commitment to reform but firmly opposing proposals that would undoubtedly have improved the day-to-day workings of the organisation both in the field and at headquarters. This became particularly clear when, in May 2006, Kofi Annan's proposals for some perfectly sensible and long overdue management reforms – addressing, inter alia, disabling features of the UN's personnel and budget practices and the issue of how the UN could make better use of information and communications technologies[73] – were voted down by the General Assembly, which chose to view the proposals as a 'power grab by the developed world'.[74] The divisions and suspicion expressed themselves again a year later, in March 2007, when three weeks of negotiations within the Peacekeeping Committee broke down without agreement and the NAM caucus, led by Morocco, stormed out amid accusations of a US attempt to force through unacceptable changes to the session's final text. For a committee with a record of producing fairly anodyne and uncontroversial reports, it was an unusual end to its annual session.

The intensification of political infighting among key member states, while reflecting the international politics of the time, was also stimulated by the manner in which the reform process was conceived, specifically by the importance attached by Annan to the subject of Security Council reform. This, one might suppose, ought not to have prevented progress in other areas. The difficulty was that throughout the process, the secretary-general and his closest advisers urged member states not to disaggregate Annan's set of proposals but to treat them instead 'as a single package'.[75] This approach to UN reform was consistent with Annan's belief in the need for radical reform. As a strategy aimed at achieving concrete results, however, it was ill-advised and ran very much counter to the historical experience of UN reform efforts.[76] One of its consequences was to encourage long-standing aspirants to permanent Security Council membership – Germany, India, Japan and Brazil (a group of countries known in this context as the G4) – to concentrate their diplomatic attention, not on the day-to-day operations of the organisation, including its peacebuilding activities (to which all four have been important contributors), but on their campaign for Council membership; campaigns which stood very little chance of success but which did have the effect of generating, as widely predicted, 'further disharmony among states'.[77]

The history of the PBC since the World Summit and its formal establishment in December 2005 – the third phase in the commission's evolution alluded to above – has inevitably been coloured by the political backdrop of the time. Most fundamentally, and indeed worryingly, as India's representative to the UN told the General Assembly in February 2007, the PBC has found it difficult to define precisely what 'the body would do and how it would go about achieving its goals'.[78] Though it is couched in diplomatic language, the Indian statement reveals the frustrations that have attended the early life of the PBC, with the permanent representative euphemistically calling for a 'more result-oriented discourse', 'a more forward-looking frame of mind' and 'a larger sense of overarching purpose' to the meetings of the Organisational Committee. Addressing the General Assembly on the same subject in October 2007, India's representative repeated his call for 'greater efforts to move beyond debating issues of process to implementing measures', and for a focus on 'the real purpose of the PBC'.[79] In late 2008, echoing the private views of others, he was again calling for a renewed effort to 'make the PBC relevant to the countries that it seeks to assist'.[80]

The very fact that the PBC was created by a concurrent resolution of the Security Council and the General Assembly and is now also uneasily linked to ECOSOC is testimony to the deep tensions among member states, as is the commission's size.[81] It is of course possible to view, as some have, the equal role given to the General Assembly and Security Council in the creation and now presumably also the workings of the PBC as giving the body greater 'democratic legitimacy'.[82] In a similar vein, Jayantha Dhanapala, Sri Lankan diplomat and one-time aspirant to the secretary-generalship, has suggested that the PBC 'represents a synthesis of several bodies in the UN system and augurs well for concrete, coordinated action' among them.[83] Sadly, there is very little historical evidence to support this view; indeed, if any law or rule can be inferred from the history of UN reform, it is that 'intergovernmental bodies tend to be enlarged until they become dysfunctional'.[84] In this regard, the role of the General Assembly raises certain concerns. As the HLP noted with a welcome dose of candour, the role and relevance of the Assembly have long been undermined by its 'unwieldy and static agenda' and its failure 'to reach closure on issues', resulting in resolutions that are 'repetitive, obscure or inapplicable, thus diminishing the credibility of the body'.[85] The panel rightly added, however, that there are no 'procedural fixes' to this state of affairs, and 'making the General Assembly a more effective instrument than it is now … can only be achieved if its Members show a sustained determination to put behind them the approach which they have applied hitherto'.[86] There is at the moment very little evidence to nourish the hope that this might happen.

It would be wrong to attribute the difficulties encountered in working out acceptable arrangements for the UN's new peacebuilding architecture entirely to the internecine politics of member states. The Secretariat and its wider bureaucracy of agencies and bodies clearly also have an interest in the new creation, something which affects the PBSO in particular. The office's official role is straightforward enough: to provide support to 'the Peacebuilding Commission and catalyz[e] the UN System, on behalf of the secretary-general, and [partner] with external actors to develop peacebuilding strategies, marshal resources and enhance international coordination', all the while undertaking these tasks on the basis of '[its] function as a knowledge centre for lessons learned and good practices on peacebuilding'.[87] While the secretary-general has been careful to stress to the organisation's varied agencies that the new office will not duplicate existing capacities, the history of earlier management reforms leaves considerable room for scepticism about the ability of the PBSO to secure the 'necessary cooperation from UN agencies and departments, including offices in the field'.[88] Specifically, like other entities created outside the larger, more operationally oriented Departments of Peacekeeping Operations and Political Affairs, the peacebuilding office is likely to be viewed with suspicion by those departments. Indeed, it may well suffer a fate similar to that of the Strategic Planning Unit, also created within the Executive Office of the Secretary-General, which has never been able to develop the role that its original champions had envisaged. Specialised agencies such as the UN Development Programme, which are answerable to their boards on which, of course, sit donor countries (ensuring that politics, as always, comes in through the back door), are also bound to want to protect their accumulated powers and freedom of action within the system.[89] The staff of the PBSO must be aware of the bureaucratic forces that militate against their office assuming a truly effective role. In what sounded more like a plea than an analytical observation, then-head of the PBSO Carolyn McAskie stated in November 2007 that 'if the office is not operational, it must be accepted by all players that the strategic process which it leads must have operational implications for the departments, programmes and agencies ... If not, we will not meet the test implicit in the creation of the new peacebuilding entities.'[90]

The PBC: an assessment and some wider implications
Realism about achievable goals
It is possible to be deeply pessimistic about the prospects for the Peacebuilding Commission, a body whose inaugural session was boldly presented as 'a historic milestone in global efforts to help countries avert a relapse into bloodshed after emerging from conflict'.[91] Indeed, four years after its creation, the indications are that the intensely political process of translating a broad and general commitment into specific institutions and mechanisms has, by providing new arenas for conflict and political infighting, primarily served to reinforce divisions and tensions within the UN body politic. Worse still, given that the UN has a dismal record of shutting down inefficient and moribund parts of its sprawling system, a dysfunctional and

irredeemably politicised PBC may end up working against the original objective of greater 'system-wide coherence' by providing new blocking mechanisms for effective action in the field. To leave this as an unqualified conclusion, however, *may* as yet prove too harsh. There are a few reasons for this.

There is, in the first instance, nothing unusual about bold and ambitious ideas for UN reform undergoing modifications, often of a drastic kind, in response to political realities. Indeed, there is often a profound sense of unreality to many of the writings that bemoan the failure of statesmen to implement imaginative, far-reaching and idealistic blueprints for UN reform. This sense of unreality was plainly evident in much of the commentary surrounding the outcome of the 2005 World Summit. The story of the PBC is, arguably, unusual in that the political circumstances under which the proposal was launched and its details negotiated by member states were particularly unfavourable, and were not helped by the 'big bang' approach to UN reform adopted by the Secretariat. Against this, the establishment and limited achievements to date of the PBC, Peacebuilding Fund and the PBSO are themselves noteworthy. More concretely, there is also some evidence to suggest that the PBC has helped to 'galvanise political international support for the peacebuilding priorities of countries on the Commission's agenda'.[92]

Beyond this, any grounds for optimism must start with the oft-forgotten recognition that away from the summit meetings and grandstanding in New York, the UN still goes about its core day-to-day business, and this includes an unprecedented number of civilian and military personnel deployed in a peacebuilding capacity. There are two ways in which the creation of the PBC and its associated bodies may still assist their deployment.

The first relates to the issue of funding and the marshalling of resources. For reasons touched on above, the UN and peacebuilding more generally have long suffered from a lack of flexible funding mechanisms.[93] To address this, the Peacebuilding Fund was set up as a standing multi-donor trust fund to 'support interventions of direct and immediate relevance to the peacebuilding process and contribute towards addressing critical gaps in that process, in particular in areas for which no other funding mechanism is available'.[94] The fund is small, but pledges have been met quickly and the evolving rules governing disbursement – including under the fund's so-called 'emergency window' – ought to improve the responsiveness of missions to developments on the ground and enable so-called 'catalytic' funding.[95] The initial funding target was $250 million and by mid 2009 around $310m had been committed, of which just under $140m has been allocated.[96] According to one assessment, the PBC has already been 'instrumental in generating crucial initial funds for Sierra Leone and Burundi'.[97]

The second and potentially more significant reason to welcome the creation of the PBC is that it ought to encourage, within the UN and among its agencies, the habit of thinking in strategic terms. There is a subtle but important difference between this and actually acting strategically. What the PBC in effect seeks to address is what in military parlance is known as the 'operational level of war', that is, the level at 'which campaigns and major operations are planned, conducted, and sustained to accomplish strategic objectives'.[98] Strategy is, or should in theory be, set in the Security Council and this is precisely why – given the divisions that often exist within that body owing to its intensely political nature – proper strategic direction is always bound to be a weakness in UN operations. That said, thinking in strategic terms, even if it only means harmonising disparate activities and directing them towards some common objective, is still enormously important for a 'system' as fragmented and disjointed as that of the UN, where key parts – notably the Bretton Woods institutions – are unaccustomed or, worse still, resistant to consulting across bureaucratic boundaries.

Wider implications for international peacebuilding and grounds for scepticism

For all this, the creation of the PBC and its associated bodies, its history to date and its current functioning do nonetheless point to wider and, in the end, critical limitations or underlying challenges – of a practical and, above all, political nature – that will continue to shape the quality and character of international responses to 'post-conflict' societies. Three such challenges, in many ways inseparable from one another, emerge from the discussion above. Although the context here is the UN, these also apply, though necessarily in a different form, to the many regional organisations and individual countries that have taken an active interest in peacebuilding in the post-Cold War era. In summary, the challenges are:

- the state-centric and process-oriented approach to dealing with the challenges of peacebuilding among member states;
- the continuing lack of relevant analytical capacity within the UN system necessary for strategic direction and differentiation among peacebuilding objectives; and
- an international political context in which divisions both among major powers and between the global North and South have become more acute over the past decade, further complicating efforts to fashion an effective response to specific and general peacebuilding challenges.

Each of these, and especially the ways in which they are connected, requires further elaboration.

The workings of the PBC in New York have been mired in state-centric formalism from the outset and an inordinate amount of time has been spent focusing on 'procedures and working methods', especially those of the main and unwieldy standing body, the Organisational Committee.[99] Indeed, the meetings of that committee have, in time-honoured UN fashion, been bogged down with procedural issues relating to the selection of committee members, and close observers claim that the sessions themselves have now been 'reduced to little more than rubber-stamping'.[100] There are profound political reasons for this, as member states often position themselves carefully on seemingly technical or procedural matters in order to signal their views on what are considered more fundamental issues. In particular, and as stressed above, the global South – with strong support from China and, increasingly, Russia – remains, for a mixture of reasons, deeply attached to the principle of sovereign equality, and is acutely sensitive to any perceived threat to it and its corollary, the principle of non-interference in the internal affairs of states. Thus, the 'cumbersome procedural regulations governing civil-society participation in Organisational Committee meetings',[101] for example, are only partly the result of any inherent difficulty in finding suitable mechanisms for interaction; they stem as much from the concerns of member states about the principle of engaging with non-state actors. There is, in short, a heavy state-centric bias in the approach to dealing with peacebuilding issues in New York; an at times debilitating attachment to formal procedures and the trappings of sovereignty leading to a focus on process over substantive issues. The historical and more contemporary reasons for this, as discussed above, are well known, and there is of course a long history of using 'the stage machinery of the United Nations as a substitute for action'.[102] But there is a wider price to pay for this approach, which brings us to the second limitation alluded to above.

The focus on process has meant that no systematic effort has gone into developing the kind of analytical capacity that would allow the UN to approach individual peacebuilding environments in terms of the contextual categories set out in Chapter 1 of this book, that is, by seeking to acquire a deeper understanding of the historical context and cultural specificities of zones of conflict, their regional dimensions and state–society relations, and, above all, the political economy of war and peace and the insights it offers into informal power structures and conflict dynamics on the ground. The absence of this capacity (or even just of mechanisms for tapping into knowledge outside the UN system) is one reason why the setting of strategic priorities and the coordination of peacebuilding efforts – the single most important justification for revamping the peacebuilding architecture at the UN in the first place – is proving so very hard.[103]

The principal mechanisms that exist for setting strategic priorities are the Integrated Peacebuilding Strategies that have been developed for individual countries, and the work that goes on in the country-specific configurations of the PBC. The first set of agreements on the development of such 'integrated strategies' was reached in February 2007 for Sierra Leone and Burundi. Since then, two further countries, Guinea–Bissau and the CAR, have been added to the agenda, and others are being considered. On paper, these developments are to be welcomed, but in practice, the work of the country-specific configurations – while possibly useful in simply drawing attention to the countries in question – have only served to highlight problems stemming from the obsession with process and procedures and the lack of 'resources and analytical capacity to closely read political dynamics on the ground, resulting in insufficient attention to local context'.[104] In the case of Guinea–Bissau, peacebuilding priorities include 'security-sector reform, wealth generation and modernisation of public administration'; a set of priorities that gives a whole new meaning to the saying that the devil is in the detail.[105] The problem is that there are few mechanisms, little capacity and not much apparent will, to engage with those details.[106] There is a similar sense of unreality about the PBC's priorities for the CAR, a country that has been described as not so much a 'failed' as a 'phantom state'[107] – something which no doubt helps to explain why the PBC found, in May 2009, that the country had not received 'sufficient tax receipts to cover its security needs, the regular functioning of State services or debt payments'.[108] As one official closely involved and sympathetic to the original ambitions for the PBC and, especially, for its country-specific work noted in mid 2009: 'My big fear is that a combination of the focus on small countries and being too process-oriented, in terms of overdoing it on visits and line-by-line negotiation of documents but not politically strong in terms of dealing with thorny issues head on, will reduce the Commission, over time, to the status of an ECOSOC Commission with little real power and a lot of time for talk and report-making'.[109] Equally problematic, however, as the work of the country-specific configurations has already shown, is what has been highlighted as a long-standing 'built-in bias to work with state-like mechanisms' on the part of the 'UN system, international financial institutions, and bilateral donors', a tendency that in many cases will further diminish their potential role in supporting meaningful peacebuilding initiatives on the ground.[110]

Underlying all of this, of course, is politics – at the UN, within the UN bureaucracy and within the larger international system. It has already been stressed that the history of the PBC from original conception to current incarnation was indelibly marked by the conviction among developing countries that industrialised Western countries, above all the US, were seeking to 'hijack' the UN to serve their own purposes. The strength of this conviction has not abated since the World Summit of 2005. Indeed, quite the opposite: developing countries have strongly and unqualifiedly reaffirmed their views on the sanctity of the principles of sovereign equality and the non-intervention rule, a position that has been reflected in their obvious and apparently growing unease with the notion of a 'Responsibility to Protect' (R2P). Formally adopted, like the PBC, by member states at the 2005 World Summit, the R2P is now widely seen by developing countries as a subterfuge for increasing Western influence in the organisation. This view was bluntly encapsulated in the opening statement to the Ministerial Meeting of the NAM Coordinating Bureau of May 2006 given by then-Prime Minister of Malaysia Abdullah Ahmad Badawi: 'New concepts and doctrines have been foisted on us, including such notions as "humanitarian intervention", "responsibility to protect" and "pre-emptive war", among others. All of these pose a challenge to traditional and universally accepted concepts enshrined in the UN charter ... We should strongly oppose any attempts at eroding them.'[111] The vein of scepticism, indeed of downright resistance, among the majority of UN member states towards the R2P was plainly evident in the UN General Assembly's 'thematic dialogue' on the subject in July 2009.[112] Badawi's and other statements are characteristic of an undifferentiated approach to – and, at one level, an unsophisticated understanding of – the 'West' or the 'global North'. Even so, there is little doubt that many developing countries have come firmly to believe, and not without some real basis in developments over the past decade, that 'Western countries want to use the UN to prescribe justice within borders, to reach deep into the domestic jurisdiction of other states, while preserving the status quo order among states'.[113] The joint statement by the African Union at its summit in Libya in July 2009 declaring the organisation's intention not to cooperate with the International Criminal Court in its pursuit of Sudan's President Omar al-Bashir reflects the same underlying sentiment.

In asserting their positions on this issue with such force and clarity, the NAM and G77 have undoubtedly been encouraged by the noticeably more assertive positions taken in defence of the principles of sovereignty and non-intervention by Russia and China over the past three years, permanent members of the Security Council whose explanatory statements and positions on a series of specific issues since early 2007 – Myanmar, Zimbabwe and Sri Lanka in particular – plainly and unequivocally distance them from what some had hoped was an emerging post-Cold War normative consensus around humanitarian engagement within states.[114] In the case of Russia, this greater assertiveness must be seen as part and parcel of a foreign policy orientation under Presidents Putin and Medvedev 'dominated by the effort to reverse the substantial decline of the 1980s and 1990s and to lay the internal basis for a return to real (as opposed to symbolic) status as a great power'.[115]

These are not, lest that be assumed, side issues marginal to this book's central concerns. They are crucial considerations, as they suggest that the international political context and the normative consensus that was thought to exist in favour of more intrusive involvement in the sphere of jurisdiction of member states – 'thought' because adopting the language and signing up to broad statements of principle never translated into a genuine acceptance of normative positions on the part of Russia or China,[116] let alone of the wider membership of the UN – have become less conducive to the kind of peacebuilding activity and ambition that has been a distinctive feature of the post-Cold War era. Even if peacebuilding operations continue to be authorised by the Security Council at the impressive rate that they have in recent years, the impact of power-political and national-interest considerations on those operations is likely to become more pronounced. Evidence of this can be seen in the developments in Kosovo in the run-up to and since its declaration of independence in February 2008, which highlighted deep divisions between Russia and Western powers.[117]

CONCLUSION

Addressing the UN Security Council in May 2008, Lakhdar Brahimi, among the most thoughtful and experienced of practitioners in the peacebuilding field, cautioned against putting together '"template" missions that set out complex and ambitious tasks for imagined armies of expert civilians who are to carry out the same laundry list of tasks in dramatically different post-conflict settings'.[1] Brahimi's words of warning draw attention to two themes that have resurfaced regularly throughout this book.

While post-Cold War commitments to transforming and reshaping war-afflicted societies have sometimes too easily and too cynically been dismissed as mere expressions of self-interest on the part of Western governments, the record of outside involvement in peacebuilding is a cautionary tale, calling for greater humility and realism before the task than that which has often informed the deliberations of policymakers, especially in the West. In part this is because political will and resources, including Brahimi's 'imagined armies of civilian experts', have tended to be in short supply, resulting in a persistent tension between available means and desired ends. When to this are added the deep divisions and limited normative consensus that exist within the wider international community about the 'new interventionism' of which the growth of peace-building is a notable expression, the limits to what can be done by external means alone to transform or re-engineer war-torn societies become still more apparent. The politics of the UN Peacebuilding Commission discussed above and, more generally, the record of Security Council politics over the past three years suggest that those divisions are, if anything, becoming more pronounced.

This is not to suggest that there have been no successes in post-Cold War attempts to build peace after war, or that the efforts of external actors to assist in war-to-peace transitions are doomed to failure. Mozambique, a country that has not figured prominently in this book, has witnessed nearly two decades of peace, steady economic growth and four multi-party elections. While Cambodia today falls well short of the standards of a mature liberal democracy, the UN's transitional authority there in the early 1990s helped to set it on a path of progress that has marked a sharp break with the country's bloody and turbulent past. The degree, however, to which both of these comparative 'successes' still fall short of original peacebuilding ambitions brings us to the second theme alluded to above.

Post-conflict environments are indeed often 'dramatically different' from one another, and the sources of those differences need to be much better understood by outsiders wishing to assist in the consolidation of peace. The post-Cold War experience of peacebuilding surveyed in these pages points to five issues or broad sets of challenges – of a conceptual as well as a practical nature – that merit more systematic attention from governments and international organisations attempting to assist countries emerging from war.

The need for sensitivity to the historical and cultural context within which peacebuilding takes place

In the planning and conduct of peacebuilding activities, greater attention needs to be given to the effects that *any* outside intervention, and particularly a protracted foreign military presence, is likely to have in nourishing nationalism, stimulating local resistance and influencing the psychological environment of a post-conflict society. In practice, this requires the development of both the analytical capacity and the organisational structures within governments and international organisations needed to enable a deeper understanding of the historical and cultural specificities of conflict zones. It also places a premium on the careful recruitment of personnel for missions, especially heads of mission, force commanders and their senior staffs, to ensure that peacebuilders possess the special skills and awarenesses – political, cultural, linguistic and otherwise – that a mission requires.

The need to understand the multiple and overlapping sources of violence in post-conflict territories

Establishing security and stabilising post-war environments – an urgent and overriding priority at the outset of any mission – demands a differentiated understanding of the varieties and sources of violence that characterise post-conflict settings. This involves not only an awareness of historical context and, in particular, of the local or 'micro-foundations' of violence, but also an appreciation of how different kinds of violence – political, economic, criminal and culturally embedded – overlap and often become increasingly difficult to distinguish on the ground. Of special and growing importance in the post-Cold War era is the challenge posed by criminal violence and organised crime in many post-conflict settings. Symbiotic relationships between political elites and criminal groups – formed during war and, in recent times, frequently aided by the emergence of a new breed of transnational criminal actors – do not simply disappear as and when an armed conflict formally ends. This is because post-conflict settings provide what are, in many ways, ideal enabling environments for a range of criminal activities, notably drug trafficking and the other criminal trades linked to it. In periods of transition from war to peace, such environments have offered conditions favourable not only to the maintenance of ties formed in wartime, but also to their proliferation and flourishing, something that has in turn stymied other peacebuilding efforts. The answer to the challenge that these developments pose cannot, however, be reduced simply to one of 'combating crime'. For one, resorting to what outsiders recognise and label as crime may, for people in desperate need and extreme circumstances, be part of a coping or survival strategy. Moreover, as stressed above, attempts to meet the challenge posed by organised crime in post-conflict settings must proceed from a nuanced understanding of its roots and functions in the local community, including the degree of legitimacy it may enjoy. Identifying those nuances requires a political-economy approach to the problems of armed conflict and peacebuilding.

The importance of strengthening local governance structures and clarifying relations with the centre
The extent to which the governance structures put in place and promoted by outsiders are viewed as legitimate by former adversaries in a post-conflict setting, neighbouring states and the international community is critical to the success of any peacebuilding endeavour. As discussed above, the importance of generating legitimacy at the local level – by working alongside and encouraging 'organic' local governance initiatives at district, municipal and even neighbourhood levels – as

distinct from a single-minded focus on central government, has in many cases been badly neglected. The two should not, however, be thought of as irreconcilable alternatives; rather, it is a question of working out the appropriate relationship and balance between them. As Matt Bryden notes, one potential 'drawback to an emphasis on local-level governance in post-conflict reconstruction ... [is] that effective local-level solutions may eventually be destabilized by subsequent national-level decisions'. Thus, the real challenge lies in 'ensuring that national-level arrangements are informed – and to some extent shaped by – governance developments at the local level'.[2]

The importance of DDR, armed groups and their political reintegration

For large numbers of regular and irregular soldiers, the immediate aftermath of war involves a difficult transition from military service to an uncertain future marked by limited employment opportunities, the loss of social status and economic privileges and, in many cases, hostility from civil society. That transition does not end with the formal end of a DDR process, however well-organised and executed this may be. As political scientist Anders Nilsson stresses in relation to armed groups in the DRC and Sierra Leone:

> The disarmament and demobilisation of armed groups does not constitute the definite turning point in the transition from war to peace ... even if formal command structures disappear with demobilisation, informal military networks and loyalties continue to thrive between ex-combatant communities, former mid-level commanders ... warlords and even old regional allies.[3]

Of particular importance to security and stability in the early post-war phase are those who stand to lose most from the end of conflict. Among these, individuals and units associated with the security and military-intelligence apparatuses of former belligerents require special attention. Not only their socio-economic but above all their *political* reintegration after conflict – broadly conceived to cover more than simply the formation of political parties – must be an urgent priority in any peace-building effort.[4]

The importance of civil–military relations and clarity of objectives in peacebuilding

Discussion of civil–military relations in peacebuilding and post-conflict operations has tended to revolve around the question of how best to improve the quality of cooperation between the military and civilian components of a mission. Clearly, this remains an important aspect of the 'civil–military challenge', whether the context is that of a donor country, an international organisation or a mission in the field. Dysfunctional command-and-control arrangements; the clash of organisational sub-cultures; the failure to harmonise and coordinate policies; fear, felt by humanitarian agencies and military establishments alike, of the effects that enforced operational proximity will have on their organisational ethos and identity, all continue – to a greater or lesser degree – to bedevil civil–military relations on the ground. Measures to address such tensions – for example through the UN's advocacy of fully integrated missions – have only been partially successful. Ultimately, however, the key to improving civilian and military cooperation on the ground lies in clarity of political objectives at the highest level and, with it, institutional mechanisms for translating those objectives into a set of realisable goals for civilians and soldiers in the field. Finding the right mechanisms, and generating sufficient bureaucratic and political will to make the process work, remains a major challenge.

*   *   *

Underlying each of these challenges is a more fundamental point. What has aptly been described as the 'mechanical metaphor',[5] which has, both explicitly and implicitly, dominated much of the Western policy discourse on 'state failure' – the superficially persuasive idea that states collapse or fall apart and can then be put back together again – is a poor conceptual aid to thinking about the challenges of peacebuilding. When presented in these terms, the idea of a 'failed state' is often, in Gérard Prunier's words, little more than a 'stereotyped category … more relevant to the Western way of thinking than to the realities [it is] supposed to address'.[6] War-torn 'post-conflict' societies in which the distinction between 'peace' and 'war' is blurred do not collapse into complete anarchy. Alternative systems of coping, even governance, emerge that are built around bonds of loyalty, trust and mutual interest at a local level. While these represent a form of adaptation to extreme circumstances and may also have violence built into them, they will also have deep historical and cultural roots. Understanding them is likely to be a more useful starting point from which to begin to consider the challenges of peacebuilding than 'template missions' and the idea of a clean slate on which the future can be written.

GLOSSARY

ACABQ	UN Advisory Committee on Administrative and Budgetary Questions
ADFL	Alliance of Democratic Forces for the Liberation of Congo-Zaire
AFRC	Armed Forces Revolutionary Council (Sierra Leone)
CAR	Central African Republic
CPA	Coalition Provisional Authority (Iraq)
DS	Dasharvna Sigurnost (Bulgarian security service)
DDR	disarmament, demobilisation and reintegration
DRC	Democratic Republic of the Congo
ECOMOG	Economic Community of West African States Monitoring Group
ECOSOC	UN Economic and Social Council
ECOWAS	Economic Community of West African States
FARDC	Forces Armées de la République Démocratique du Congo (Democratic Republic of the Congo Armed Forces)
FDLR	Forces Démocratiques de Libération du Rwanda (Democratic Liberation Forces of Rwanda)
G77	Group of 77
HLP	High-Level Panel on Threats, Challenges and Change
HNP	Haitian National Police
ICSD	International Council on Security and Development
IEMF	Interim Emergency Multinational Force (DRC)

ISAF	International Security Assistance Force (Afghanistan)
MINUSTAH	UN Stabilisation Mission in Haiti
MONUC	UN Mission in the Democratic Republic of the Congo
MPLA	Movimento Popular de Libertação de Angola (Popular Movement for the Liberation of Angola)
NAM	Non-Aligned Movement
PBC	UN Peacebuilding Commission
PBSO	UN Peacebuilding Support Office
R2P	Responsibility to Protect
RCD	Rassemblement Congolais pour la Démocratie (Congolese Rally for Democracy)
RUF	Revolutionary United Front (Sierra Leone)
SLA	Sierra Leone Army
SSR	security-sector reform
UNAMSIL	UN Mission in Sierra Leone
UNITA	União Nacional para a Independência Total de Angola (National Union for the Total Independence of Angola)
UNTAC	UN Transitional Authority in Cambodia
UNTAES	UN Operation in Eastern Slavonia

NOTES

Introduction

1   For a treatment of this issue, see Adam Roberts and Dominik Zaum, *Selective Security: War and the United Nations Security Council since 1945*, Adelphi Paper 395 (Abingdon: Routledge for the IISS, 2008).

2   In addition to a long-standing, though now scaled down, UN presence, the Balkans 'peacebuilding laboratory' has housed five Organisation for Security and Cooperation in Europe (OSCE) missions, two EU Police Missions and two major military deployments by NATO. NATO's Stabilisation Force in Bosnia (SFOR), which deployed following the Dayton Peace Accord, was replaced in December 2004 by an EU military operation, EUFOR, whose troop strength, initially above 6,000, was just above 2,000 in March 2009.

3   Stephen Jackson, 'The UN Operation in Burundi (ONUB) – Political and Strategic Lessons Learned', External Study for UN Department of Peacekeeping Operations Best Practices Section, July 2006, p. 1.

4   League of Nations activities that would have been covered by the UN's broad definition of 'peacebuilding' include its role in administering the Saar and the city of Danzig following the Treaty of Versailles, its involvement in large-scale refugee repatriation in Russia in 1920–21, and the efforts it made to address the consequences of continued violence between Greece and Turkey in 1922–26. The League also established a Minorities Section and undertook a series of investigations aimed at resolving disputes between states. For an overview of the League's role as a precursor to the UN in the field of peacekeeping, which persuasively argues that 'the League deserves much more credit than it generally receives', see Alan James, 'The Peacekeeping Role of the League of Nations', *International Peacekeeping*, vol. 6, no. 1, Spring 1999, pp. 155–60.

5   Michael Doyle, Ian Johnstone and Robert Orr, 'Introduction', in M. Doyle, I. Johnstone and R. Orr (eds), *Keeping the Peace: Multinational UN Operations in Cambodia and El Salvador* (Cambridge: Cambridge University Press, 1997), p. 2. Doyle, Johnstone and Orr made this observation in relation to the UN's Cambodia operation in 1992 and 1993,

but it accurately captures the broad aims and aspirations of other missions as well.

6 Renata Dwan and Sharon Wiharta, 'Multilateral Peace Missions: Challenges of Peacebuilding', in *SIPRI Yearbook 2005* (Oxford: Oxford University Press, 2005), p. 146.

7 James Mayall (ed.), *The New Interventionism, 1991–94* (Cambridge: Cambridge University Press, 1997).

8 For discussion of whether or not a 'solidarist' consensus has emerged in international relations, see Rosemary Foot, John Lewis Gaddis and Andrew Hurrell (eds), *Order and Justice in International Relations* (Oxford: Oxford University Press, 2003), especially the Introduction and Chapter 1.

9 UN General Assembly, '2005 World Summit Outcome', A/60/L.1, 15 September 2005, paragraph 139. Thomas Weiss, for example, has argued that 'with the possible exception of the 1948 Convention on Genocide, no idea has moved faster in the international normative arena than "the responsibility to protect"'. Thomas Weiss, *Humanitarian Intervention* (Cambridge: Polity Press, 2007), p. 1.

10 David Curran and Tom Woodhouse, 'Cosmopolitan Peacekeeping and Peacebuilding in Sierra Leone: What can Africa Contribute?', *International Affairs*, vol. 83, no. 6, November 2007, pp. 1,055–70.

11 Adam Roberts, 'Humanitarian Principles in International Politics in the 1990s', in Humanitarian Studies Unit, ECHO (ed), *Reflections on Humanitarian Action: Principles, Ethics and Contradictions* (London: Pluto Press, 2001), p. 23.

12 For an excellent assessment of contemporary patterns of intervention in world politics which strikes a careful balance between interest-based and normative motivations, see S. Neil MacFarlane, *Intervention in Contemporary World Politics*, Adelphi Paper 350 (Oxford: Oxford University Press for the IISS, 2002).

13 Dwan and Wiharta, 'Multilateral Peace Missions: Challenges of Peacebuilding'.

14 See *European Military Capabilities: Building Armed Forces for Modern Operations*, IISS Strategic Dossier (London: IISS, 2008), pp. 13 and 117; and Nora Bensahel, 'Organising for Nation-Building', *Survival*, vol. 49, no. 2, Summer 2007, pp. 43–76.

15 Kirsten Soder, 'Multilateral Peace Operations in 2008', *SIPRI Yearbook 2009* (Oxford: Oxford University Press, 2009), p. 117. On the steady growth in peace operations since 2005, including non-UN missions, see also the annual review of global peace operations prepared by the Center for International Cooperation in New York. According to the centre's most recent survey, the 'global peace-operations footprint' increased by 8.7% in 2008. *Annual Review of Global Peace Operations 2009* (Boulder, CO: Lynne Rienner for the Center on International Cooperation, 2009).

16 *Annual Review of Global Peace Operations 2008* (Boulder, CO: Lynne Rienner for the Center on International Cooperation, 2008), pp. 101–2. The proposed strength of the EU force in Chad and the CAR is 3,700.

17 'NATO After Istanbul', NATO Public Diplomacy Division, no date.

18 'Testimony of General John P. Abizaid, Commander, United States Central Command, before the 108th Congress Senate Armed Services Committee',

25 September 2003, available at GlobalSecurity.org, p. 4.

19 For an overview of some of these efforts, see Stewart Patrick and Kaysie Brown, *Greater Than the Sum of its Parts? Assessing 'Whole of Government' Approaches to Fragile States* (New York: International Peace Academy, 2007).

20 UN General Assembly, '2005 World Summit Outcome', A/Res/60/1, 24 October 2005. The origins and role of the PBC are discussed more fully in Chapter 3.

21 Philip Windsor, 'The Future of Strategic Studies', unpublished paper, no date, p. 1.

22 Windsor, 'The Future of Strategic Studies', p. 1.

23 For an idea of the variety of meanings and connotations that the term 'peacebuilding' has acquired, see also Michael Barnett, Hunjoon Kim, Madalene O'Donnell and Laura Sitea, 'Peacebuilding: What is in a Name?', *Global Governance*, vol. 13, no. 1, January–March 2007, pp. 35–58.

24 United Nations, 'An Agenda for Peace', Report of the Secretary-General, A/47/277-S/24111, 17 June 1992, paragraph 21.

25 For the most recent such debate in the Security Council, held in May 2008 at the initiative of the UK, see Security Council 5895th Meeting, UN Document S/PV.5895, 20 May 2008.

26 United Nations, 'Annual Report of the Secretary-General on the Work of the Organization', A/53/1, 1998, paragraph 65.

27 Elizabeth M. Cousens, 'Introduction', in Elizabeth M. Cousens and Chetan Kumar (eds), *Peacebuilding as Politics: Cultivating Peace in Fragile Societies* (Boulder, CO: Lynne Rienner, 2001), p. 10.

28 *Ibid.*, p. 13.

29 Mats Berdal, 'Beyond Greed and Grievance – and not too soon…', *Review of International Studies*, vol. 31, 2005, pp. 687–98.

30 United Nations, 'Report of the Panel on United Nations Peace Operations', A/55/305, 21 August 2000, paragraph 13.

31 In certain areas of policy intervention – a prime example being that of DDR – the seemingly logical commitment to a sequential approach (i.e. disarmament *followed by* demobilisation *followed by* reintegration) has often run counter to the political dynamics of the post-conflict environment, with destabilising consequences. This is discussed more fully in Chapter 2.

32 Again, this is at odds with the position found in some of the peacebuilding literature. Taisier M. Ali and Robert Matthews, for example, introduce a series of African case studies with the observation that 'the success or failure of peacebuilding is not likely to be determined in the two to three years that follow a negotiated settlement'. The view taken here is that while success may not be determined during this period, post-Cold War experience suggests clearly that failure may. Taisier M. Ali and Robert O. Matthews (eds), *Durable Peace: Challenges for Peacebuilding in Africa* (Toronto: University of Toronto Press, 2004).

33 One aspect of the dilemma that has received much attention in the literature is the role of elections in post-conflict environments. As Nancy Bermeo reminds us, 'elections are easily idealised as arenas in which conflicts are resolved, but they can exacerbate conflict as well'.

Post-conflict or transitional justice is another area of outside policy intervention where hard choices have had to be made, for example where the provision of amnesties has sometimes been deemed necessary for peace processes to stay afloat. Bermeo, 'What the Democratization Literature Says – or Doesn't Say – about Postwar Democratization', *Global Governance*, vol. 9, no. 2, April–June 2003, p. 165.

34 Phil Williams and John T. Picarelli, 'Combating Organized Crime in Armed Conflict', in Karen Ballentine and Heiko Nitzschke (eds), *Profiting from Peace: Managing the Resource Dimensions of Civil War* (Boulder, CO: Lynne Rienner, 2005), p. 127.

35 Cindy Fazey, 'Responding to the Opium Dilemma', in Robert I. Rothberg (ed), *Building a New Afghanistan* (Washington DC: Brookings Institution Press, 2007).

36 Private communication with government official, November 2008.

37 Ali A. Jalabi, 'Legacy of War and the Challenge of Peacebuilding', in Rothberg (ed), *Building a New Afghanistan*, p. 47. According to the UN's annual opium survey, some 8,200 tonnes of opium were produced in Afghanistan in 2007. This represents a 34% increase on 2006, and makes the country 'practically the exclusive supplier of the world's deadliest drug'. See UN Office on Drugs and Crime, 'Afghanistan Opium Survey 2007', August 2007.

38 David Spivack (ed.), 'Feasibility Study on Opium Licensing in Afghanistan for the Production of Morphine and Other Essential Medicines', commissioned by the Senlis Council, 3rd edition, January 2006, p. 22. See also 'US Policy in Afghanistan: Senlis Council Recommendations', February 2008, http://www.icosgroup.net/documents/us_policy_recommendations.pdf. (NB the International Council on Security and Development was previously known as the Senlis Council.)

39 Jalabi, 'Legacy of War and the Challenge of Peacebuilding', p. 48.

40 Conversation with government official.

41 Fazey, 'Responding to the Opium Dilemma', pp. 178–204.

42 Leszek Kolakowski, 'The Self-Poisoning of the Open Society', in *Modernity on Endless Trial* (Chicago, IL: Chicago University Press, 1990), p. 163.

43 Among the issues and challenges associated with 'post-conflict' interventions that cannot be examined in depth here, transitions from war to peace raise complex macro- and microeconomic issues relating to the reconstruction of war-torn economies. For an excellent contribution on this subject, see Gracianna del Castillo, *Rebuilding War-torn States: The Challenge of Post-Conflict Economic Reconstruction* (Oxford: Oxford University Press, 2008).

44 This point is made by Hilary Synnott, regional coordinator for the Coalition Provisional Authority in southern Iraq for six months in 2003, who has argued that 'the experience acquired by those who dealt with … Haiti, Somalia, Kosovo, Bosnia Sierra Leone, East Timor and Afghanistan, has much in common with that gained in Iraq'. Synnott, 'The Coalition Provisional Authority in Southern Iraq', unpublished paper, 2005, p. 5. The paper is an extended version of Synnott, 'State Building in Southern

Iraq', *Survival*, vol. 47, no. 2, Summer 2005. See also Synnott, *Bad Days in Basra* (London: I.B. Tauris, 2008).

45 Ioan Lewis and James Mayall, 'Somalia', in Mats Berdal and Spyros Economides (eds), *United Nations Interventionism,* *1991–2004* (Cambridge: Cambridge University Press, 2007), p. 137.

46 Hugh Seton-Watson, *Neither War nor Peace: The Struggle for Power in the Post-War World* (London: Methuen & Co, 1960), p. 13.

Chapter One

1 'A Review of Peace Operations: A Case for Change', Conflict, Security and Development Group, King's College London, 2003, p. 216.

2 Private communication, NATO, Brussels, June 2007.

3 In November 2002, UK Prime Minister Tony Blair and Foreign Secretary Jack Straw met informally with a group of academics at Downing Street to discuss the future of Iraq. One of the attendees, Charles Tripp, recalled later how the foreign secretary at the time appeared to believe that 'post-Saddam Iraq would be much like post-Soviet Russia'. Ali Allawi, who has held a number of ministerial positions in post-war Iraq, including minister of trade and minister of finance, has observed how the 'series of impractical market-inspired reforms' initiated by the Coalition Provisional Authority in 2003 were 'mostly culled from the East European model of "shock therapy", which took no account of the repercussions they engendered'. Charles Tripp, 'Militias, Vigilantes, Death Squads', *London Review of Books*, 25 January 2007, p. 30; Ali A. Allawi, *The Occupation of Iraq: Winning the War, Losing the Peace* (New Haven, CT: Yale University Press, 2007), p. 125.

4 Jeremy Black, *Rethinking Military History* (London: Routledge, 2004), p. 242.

5 'UNTAES: A Successful UN Mission in the Heart of Former Yugoslavia', UNTAES Public Affairs, no date.

6 Private interviews with UNTAES personnel, 1998. A fair and balanced assessment of the operation's achievements, which touches on this problem of measuring success, is given in Derek Boothby, 'The Political Challenges of Administering Eastern Slavonia', *Global Governance*, vol. 10, no. 1, 2004, pp. 37–51.

7 The UN Integrated Mission in Timor-Leste, technically a 'follow-on' mission consisting of some 1,600 personnel, was established by UN Security Council Resolution 1706, 25 August 2006. On the origins and nature of post-independence violence in Timor Leste, see James Scambary, 'Anatomy of a Conflict: The 2006–2007 Communal Violence in East Timor', *Conflict, Security and Development*, vol. 9, no. 2, 2009, pp. 265–85.

8 UN Security Council Resolution 1244, 10 June 1999.

9 'Many Die as Kosovo Clashes Spread', BBC News, 17 March 2004, http://news.bbc.co.uk/1/hi/world/europe/3521068.stm.

10 'Angola Unravels: The Rise and Fall of the Lusaka Peace Process', Human Rights Watch report, 1999, p. 4.

11 Tony Hodges, *Angola from Afro-Stalinism to Petro-Diamond Capitalism* (Oxford: James Currey, 2001), p. 18.

12 Alex Vines and Bereni Oruitemeka, 'Beyond Bullets to Ballots: The Reintegration of UNITA in Angola', in Mats Berdal and David Ucko (eds), *Reintegrating Armed Groups After Conflict: Politics, Violence and Transition* (London and New York: Routledge, 2009).

13 Vines and Oruitemeka, 'Beyond Bullets to Ballots: The Reintegration of UNITA in Angola', p. 199.

14 Gérard Prunier, *Africa's World War: Congo, the Rwandan Genocide, and the Making of a Continental Catastrophe* (Oxford: Oxford University Press, 2009), p. 277.

15 'Peace Agreement between the Government of Sierra Leone and the Revolutionary United Front of Sierra Leone' (Lomé Accord), Article VII (1), 3 June 1999. The January 1999 RUF and AFRC offensive – one of exceptional brutality and terror – was dubbed 'Operation No Living Thing' by the notorious RUF commander in charge, Sam Bockarie. For thoughtful assessments of the background to the Lomé Accord and the criticisms levelled at it at the time and since, see Funmi Olonisakin, *Peacekeeping in Sierra Leone: The Story of UNAMSIL* (Boulder, CO: Lynne Rienner, 2007), pp. 34–42; and Abiodun Alao and Comfort Ero, 'Cut Short for Taking Short Cuts: The Lomé Peace Agreement on Sierra Leone', *Civil Wars*, vol. 4, no. 3, 2001, pp. 117–34.

16 Adekeye Adebajo and David Keen, 'Sierra Leone', in Berdal and Economides (eds), *United Nations Interventionism, 1991–2004*, p. 257.

17 *Ibid.*, p. 258.

18 Mats Berdal, Gemma Collantes Celador and Merima Zupcevic, 'Post-Conflict Violence in Bosnia and Herzegovina, 1995–2008', paper prepared for conference on 'Post-Conflict Violence', Chr. Michelsen Institute, Bergen, Norway, 30–31 March 2009.

19 'Whither Bosnia?', International Crisis Group Report, 9 September 1998, p. 4.

20 Writing nearly a decade after the end of the war, David Harland, a senior official in the UN's Department of Peacekeeping Operations, noted that although nearly $10bn had been spent in Bosnia 'and many thousands of foreigners, military and civilian, have worked on the implementation of the Dayton Agreement … Bosnia is still far from being a self-sustaining state'. David Harland, 'Lesson for Peacemakers: What has Not Happened in Bosnia', *International Herald Tribune*, 27 January 2004.

21 Edward N. Luttwak, 'Give War a Chance', *Foreign Affairs*, vol. 78, no. 4, July–August 1999.

22 Vines and Oruitemeka, 'Beyond Bullets to Ballots: The Reintegration of UNITA in Angola', p. 205. Prunier, *Africa's World War: Congo, the Rwandan Genocide, and the Making of a Continental Catastrophe*, p. 286.

23 The endgame – for the time being at any rate – of Sri Lanka's civil war in 2009 brought home very clearly the potentially horrific cost of 'giving war a chance'. See 'UN Call for Inquiry on "Unacceptably High" Civilian Death Toll in Sri Lanka', *Guardian*, 30 May 2009; 'The Hidden Massacre', *The Times*, 29 May 2009; private communication.

24 Olonisakin, *Peacekeeping in Sierra Leone: The Story of UNAMSIL*, p. 40. Jackson at one point described RUF leader Foday

Sankoh as the 'Nelson Mandela of Sierra Leone', and was considered by many Sierra Leoneans to be unsuited to the job of mediation in view of his 'long-time friendship' with Charles Taylor of Liberia. Norimitsu Onishi, 'How the US left Sierra Leone Tangled in Curious Web', *New York Times*, 4 June 2000.

25 Tripp, 'After Saddam', *Survival*, vol. 44, no. 4, 2002, pp. 33 and 34.

26 This is the central focus of Michael Pugh and Neil Cooper with Jonathan Goodhand, *War Economies in a Regional Context* (Boulder, CO: Lynne Rienner, 2003).

27 Karen Ballentine, 'Program on Economic Agendas in Civil Wars: Final Report', International Peace Institute, April 2004, p. 6.

28 Stephen Jackson, 'Potential Difference: Internal Borderlands in Africa', in Michael Pugh, Neil Cooper and Mandy Turner (eds), *Critical Perspectives on War-transformed Economies* (Basingstoke: Palgrave, 2008), p. 329. For the work of Pugh, Cooper and Goodhand on this subject, see Pugh, Cooper and Goodhand, *War Economies in a Regional Context*.

29 This is one of the conditions for success in peace operations identified, quite rightly, by the UN's 'capstone' doctrine of 2008. See UN Department of Peacekeeping Operations, 'UN Peacekeeping Operations: Principles and Guidelines', 2008.

30 Mats Berdal, 'The UN Security Council and Peacekeeping', in Vaughan Lowe, Adam Roberts, Jennifer Welsh and Dominik Zaum (eds), *The Security Council and War: The Evolution of Thought and Practice since 1945* (Oxford: Oxford University Press, 2008), pp. 192–3.

31 Toby Dodge, *Iraq's Future: The Aftermath of Regime Change*, Adelphi Paper 372 (Abingdon: Routledge for the IISS), p. 11; Ahmed S. Hashim, *Insurgency and Counter-Insurgency in Iraq* (London: Hurst & Co., 2006), pp. 13–14.

32 Larry Diamond, 'What Went Wrong in Iraq', *Foreign Affairs*, vol. 83, no. 5, September–October 2004, p. 5.

33 This point is well made by Ali Allawi who, for this reason, is wary of the notion of an 'Iraqi national resistance'. Allawi, *The Occupation of Iraq: Winning the War, Losing the Peace*, p. 176.

34 On this important point in relation to the complex 'legacy of colonialism', see James Mayall, 'The Legacy of Colonialism', in Simon Chesterman, Michael Ignatieff and Ramesh Thakur (eds), *Making States Work: State Failure and the Crisis of Governance* (Tokyo: United Nations University Press, 2005), pp. 50–51.

35 Tripp, 'Militias, Vigilantes, Death Squads', p. 30.

36 Dodge, 'How Iraq Was Lost', *Survival*, vol. 48, no. 4, 2006–07, pp. 157–71. See also Michael Gordon and Bernard Trainor, *Cobra II – The Inside Story of the Invasion and Occupation of Iraq* (London: Atlantic Books, 2006), especially pp. 138–63.

37 Journalist and author George Packer, quoted in Dodge, 'How Iraq Was Lost', p. 161. See also Rajiv Chandrasekaran, *Imperial Life in the Emerald City: Inside Baghdad's Green Zone* (London: Bloomsbury, 2007), especially pp. 101–5.

38 Allawi, *The Occupation of Iraq: Winning the War, Losing the Peace*, p. 7. For a thoughtful comparison of the British occupation of Iraq in the 1920s and the US experience after 2003, see Dodge, 'Iraq: The Contradictions of

Exogenous State-building in Historical Perspective', *Third World Quarterly*, vol. 27, no. 1, pp. 187–200.

39 Allawi, *The Occupation of Iraq: Winning the War, Losing the Peace*, p. 10.

40 Antonio Giustozzi, *Koran, Kalashnikov and Laptop: The Neo-Taliban Insurgency in Afghanistan* (London: Hurst & Company, 2007).

41 Lieven cites one activist of the anti-Taliban Awami National Party: 'The problem is that most Pashtuns feel that to resist foreign occupation is part of what it is to follow the Pashtun Way.' See Anatol Lieven, 'The War in Afghanistan: Its Background and Future Prospects', *Conflict, Security and Development*, vol. 9, no. 3, October 2009.

42 Corelli Barnett, 'Post-conquest Civil Affairs: Comparing War's End in Iraq and in Germany', Foreign Policy Centre, February 2005, pp. 5–6.

43 Isam al-Khafaji, 'A Few Days After: State and Society in Post-Saddam Iraq', in Toby Dodge and Steven Simon (eds), *Iraq at the Crossroads: State and Society in the Shadow of Regime Change*, Adelphi Paper 354 (Oxford: Oxford University Press for the IISS, 2003), p. 83.

44 Samantha Power, *Chasing the Flame: Sergio Vieira de Mello and the Fight to Save the World* (London: Penguin Books, 2008), p. 323.

45 Kimberly Zisk Marten, *Enforcing the Peace* (New York: Columbia University Press, 2004), p. 2.

46 Isaiah Berlin, 'The Bent Twig', in Berlin, *The Crooked Timber of Humanity: Chapters in the History of Ideas* (London: John Murray, 1990), p. 248.

47 Christopher Bayly and Tim Harper, *Forgotten Wars: The End of Britain's Asian Empire* (London: Penguin Books, 2007), p. 550.

48 See Ken Menkhaus, *Somalia: State Collapse and the Threat of Terrorism*, Adelphi Paper 364 (Oxford: Oxford University Press for the IISS, 2004); Menkhaus, 'Governance Without Government in Somalia', *International Security*, vol. 31, no. 3, 2006–07. For the difficulties that outsiders have had in dealing with Somalia on its own terms in recent times and their consequences, see also Ioan M. Lewis, *A Modern History of the Somali*, 4th edition (Oxford: James Currey, 2002), pp. 262–311.

49 Stephen Ellis, 'Liberia's Warlord Insurgency', in Christopher Clapham (ed.), *African Guerrillas* (Oxford: James Currey, 1998), p. 169.

50 Douglas H. Johnson, *The Root Causes of Sudan's Civil Wars* (Oxford: James Currey, 2003), pp. xviii and 1–7.

51 Amin Saikal, *Modern Afghanistan: A History of Struggle and Survival* (London: I.B. Tauris, 2006), p. 9.

52 Sally Healy, 'Lost Opportunities in the Horn of Africa: How Conflicts Connect and Peace Agreements Unravel', Horn of Africa Group Report, Chatham House, London, 2008, p. 7.

53 Patrick Chabal and Jean-Pascal Daloz, *Africa Works: Disorder as Political Instrument* (Oxford: James Curry, 1999), p. xviii.

54 Dominique Jacquin-Berdal, 'How New are Africa's "New Wars"? A Historical Sketch', unpublished paper, 2005. See also Stephen Ellis, 'The Old Roots of Africa's New Wars', *Internationale Politik und Gesellschaft*, vol. 2, 2003.

55 Mayall, 'The Legacy of Colonialism', p. 57.

56 Charles Tilly, *The Politics of Collective Violence* (Cambridge: Cambridge University Press, 2003), p. 3.

57 Kees Koonings and Dirk Kruijt (eds), *Armed Actors: Organised Violence and*

State Failure in Latin America (London: Zed Books, 2004), pp. 156–8.

58 Ginger Thompson, 'A New Wave of Violence in Guatemala's Streets', *International Herald Tribune*, 1 January 2006; Mica Rosenberg, 'Violence Haunts Guatemala's Elections', *Time*, 3 November 2007.

59 John-Andrew McNeish and Oscar López Rivera, 'Tiro de Gracia: The Socio-Political Poetics of Violence in Post Accord Guatemala', unpublished paper for project on 'Violence in the Post-Conflict State', Chr. Michelsen Institute, Bergen, 2007, p. 4.

60 See Charles T. Call, 'The Mugging of a Success Story: Justice and Security Sector Reform in El Salvador', in Call (ed.), *Constructing Justice and Security after War* (Washington DC: United States Institute of Peace, 2007), p. 39; William Stanley, 'Business as Usual? Justice and Policing Reform in Postwar Guatemala', in *ibid.*

61 Torunn Wimpelmann, 'Patterns of Violence in Postwar Sierra Leone, Liberia and Mozambique', draft paper prepared for project on 'Violence in the Post-Conflict State', Chr. Michelsen Institute, Bergen, 2008, pp. 12 and 20; 'Crime Wave Defeats Liberia Police', BBC News, 9 July 2006, http://www.news.bbc.co.uk/go/pr/fr/-/1/hi/world/africa/5323012.stm. That said, when the period since 1992 is viewed as a whole, levels of post-conflict violence in Mozambique must be considered low in comparison to many other post-conflict settings.

62 UN Security Council, 'Report of the Secretary-General on the United Nations Stabilization Mission in Haiti', S/2007/503, 22 August 2007, paragraph 26.

63 Kieran Mitton, 'Rearmament, Remobilisation and Disintegration in Sierra Leone', unpublished paper for project on 'Conflict, Security and Development', King's College London, March 2009.

64 UN Security Council, 'Second Report of the Secretary-General on the United Nations Integrated Peacebuilding Office in Sierra Leone', S/2009/267, 22 May 2009, paragraph 2.

65 Marcus Cox, 'Bosnia and Herzegovina: The Limits of Liberal Imperialism', in Call (ed.), *Building States to Build Peace* (Boulder, CO: Lynne Rienner, 2008), p. 256.

66 Sorpong Peou, 'Violence in Post-conflict Cambodia', paper prepared for conference on 'Post-Conflict Violence', Chr. Michelsen Institute, Bergen, 30–31 March 2009, p. 7.

67 This phenomenon is identified in 'Armed Violence in Burundi: Conflict and Post-Conflict Bujumbura', in *Small Arms Survey 2007: Guns and the City* (Cambridge: Cambridge University Press, 2007), p. 221.

68 Susan Woodward, 'Do the Root Causes of Civil War Matter?', *Journal of Intervention and Statebuilding*, vol. 1, no. 2, June 2007, p. 156.

69 *Ibid.*, p. 156. The micro-foundations of violence have been highlighted above all in the work of Stathis N. Kalyvas. See Kalyvas, *The Logic of Violence in Civil Wars* (Cambridge: Cambridge University Press, 2006).

70 A good illustration of this tendency, as James Scambary has shown, is provided by the case of post-independence East Timor, where gang, politically motivated and communal violence overlapped during the so-called 'Crisis' of 2006–2007. See Scambary, 'Anatomy of a Conflict: The 2006–2007 Communal Violence in East Timor', pp. 282–5.

71 Phil Williams, 'Organized Crime and Corruption in Iraq', *International Peacekeeping* (special issue), vol. 16, no. 1, 2009, p. 116.

72 Bayly and Harper, *Forgotten Wars: The End of Britain's Asian Empire*, p. 45.

73 David Stafford, *Endgame 1945: Victory, Retribution and Liberation* (London: Abacus, 2008), p. 420.

74 *Ibid.*, p. 420.

75 Edelberto Torres-Riva, 'Insurrection and Civil War in El Salvador', in Doyle, Johnstone and Orr (eds), *Keeping the Peace: Multinational UN Operations in Cambodia and El Salvador*, p. 209.

76 Alvaro de Soto and Graciana del Castillo, 'Implementation of Comprehensive Peace Agreements: Staying the Course in El Salvador', *Global Governance*, vol. 1, no. 2, 1995, pp. 195–6. De Soto was special representative of the secretary-general to the Central American peace process and del Castillo was an economic adviser to the secretary-general. See also Joaquín M. Chávez, 'Perspectives on Demobilisation, Reintegration and Weapons Control in the El Salvador Peace Process', in *Viewpoints* (Centre for Humanitarian Dialogue), vol. 1, March 2008, p. 15.

77 De Soto and del Castillo, 'Implementation of Comprehensive Peace Agreements: Staying the Course in El Salvador', p. 195.

78 Mo Hume, 'El Salvador: The Limits of a Violent Peace', in Pugh, Cooper and Turner (eds), *Critical Perspectives on War-transformed Economies*, p. 322.

79 Michael J. Boyle, 'Explaining Strategic Violence after Wars', *Studies in Conflict and Terrorism*, vol. 32, no. 1, 2009, pp. 211–12.

80 *Ibid.*

81 *Ibid.*

82 *Ibid.* I am grateful to Michael Boyle for also sharing with me the Introduction to his forthcoming *Explaining Violence after Wars.*

83 Dodge, *Iraq's Future: The Aftermath of Regime Change*, p. 15.

84 Chávez, 'Perspectives on Demobilisation, Reintegration and Weapons Control in the El Salvador Peace Process', p. 15; and William Stanley, 'Building New Police Forces in El Salvador and Guatemala: Learning and Counter-Learning', in Tor Tanke Holm and Espen Barth Eide (eds), *Peacebuilding and Police Reform* (London: Frank Cass, 2000), pp. 118–20.

85 Albane Prophette, Claudia Paz, Jose Garcia Noval, Nieves Gomez, 'Violence in Guatemala After the Armed Conflict', paper presented to an international symposium organised by CERI, IPA and UNU, New York, June 2003, p. 7, http://www.ceri-sciencespo. com/themes/re-imaginingpeace/va/ country/guatemala_research.pdf.

86 *Ibid.*, p. 7.

87 Are Knudsen and Nasser Yasin, 'Political Violence in Post-Civil War Lebanon, 1989–2007', paper prepared for project on 'Violence in the Post-Conflict State', Chr. Michelsen Institute, Bergen, 2008, p. 2.

88 *Ibid.*, p. 26. By contrast, retributive violence and 'overt violence against civilians has been low' in the post-war period in Lebanon. *Ibid.*, p. 25.

89 David Andress, *The Terror: Civil War in the French Revolution* (London: Little, Brown, 2005), pp. 4–5.

90 Helen Graham, *The Spanish Republic at War 1936–1939* (Cambridge: Cambridge University Press, 2002), pp. 423–5. According to Francisco Salvadó, around 150,000 people were murdered after the war. Francisco J. Romero

Salvadó, *The Spanish Civil War: Origins, Course and Outcomes* (Basingstoke: Palgrave, 2005). I am grateful to Hernan Rodriguez Velasco for drawing my attention to recent research on post-Spanish Civil War violence.

91 Michael Richards, 'Violence and the Post-Conflict State in Historical Perspective: Spain, 1936–1948', paper prepared for conference on 'Post-Conflict Violence', Chr. Michelsen Institute, Bergen, 30–31 March 2009, p. 9.

92 *Ibid.*, p. 19.

93 *Ibid.*, pp. 15–18 and 34. Even in this case, as Richards notes, 'ideology' did not 'explain everything', and 'there was an important level of "privatisation" of violence in Spain'.

94 Hans Magnus Enzenberger, *Civil War* (London: Granta Books, 1994), p. 30.

95 However, as will be argued more fully in the next chapter, this is not to suggest that there is a simple or automatic relationship between high levels of unemployment and post-conflict violence.

96 Call, 'The Mugging of a Success Story: Justice and Security Sector Reform in El Salvador', p. 43; and Stanley, 'Building New Police Forces in El Salvador and Guatemala: Learning and Counter-Learning', pp. 118–19.

97 David Malone and Sebastian von Einsiedel, 'Haiti', in Berdal and Economides (eds), *United Nations Interventionism, 1991–2004*, p. 185; see also Sandra Beidas, Colin Granderson, Rachel Neild, 'Justice and Security Reform after Intervention: Haiti', in Call (ed.), *Constructing Justice and Security After War*, p. 74.

98 UN Office on Drugs and Crime, 'Transnational Organized Crime in the West African Region', 2005, pp. 30 and 19. See also '10,000 Ex-Combatants Terrorise Ordinary Citizens', Africa News Agency, 13 December 1999, http://www.reliefweb.int/rw/rwb.nsf/db900SID/OCHA-64C584; 'Liberia: Uneven Progress in Security Sector Reform', International Crisis Group Africa Report no. 148, 13 January 2009, p. 5.

99 Dodge, *Iraq's Future: The Aftermath of Regime Change*, p. 15. See also Williams, 'Organised Crime and Corruption in Iraq', pp. 123–8; and Walter Pincus, 'USAID Paper Details Security Crisis in Iraq', *Washington Post*, 17 January 2006.

100 Dodge, 'State Collapse and Identity Politics', in Markus Bouillon, David Malone and Ben Roswell (eds), *Iraq: Preventing a New Generation of Conflict* (Boulder, CO: Lynne Rienner, 2007), p. 29. See also James Glantz and Robert F. Worth, 'Attacks on Iraq Oil Industry Aid Vast Smuggling Scheme', *New York Times*, 4 June 2006.

101 Julius R. Ruff, *Violence in Early Modern Europe, 1500–1800* (Cambridge: Cambridge University Press, 2001), p. 223.

102 *Ibid.*, p. 64.

103 *Ibid.*, pp. 64–6.

104 *Ibid.*, p. 65.

105 *Ibid.*, p. 64.

106 Wimpelmann, 'Patterns of Violence in Postwar Sierra Leone, Liberia and Mozambique', p. 20.

107 UN Office of Drug Control and Crime Prevention, 'The Drug Nexus in Africa', monograph series, issue no. 1, 1999, pp. 100–101.

108 The crisis of 2000 and its consequences are discussed more fully in the next chapter.

109 Adedeji Ebo, 'The Challenges and Lessons of SSR in post-Conflict Sierra Leone', *Conflict, Security and*

Development, vol. 6, no. 4, 2006, p. 497. See also Al-Hassan Kondeh, 'Sierra Leone', in Alan Bryden, Boubacar N'Diaye, Funmi Olonisakin (eds), *Challenges of Security Sector Governance in West Africa* (Zurich: LIT Verlag GmbH & Co., 2008); private communication.

110 Georgez Nzongola-Ntalaja, *The Congo From Leopold to Kabila: A People's History* (London: Zed Books, 2002), pp. 154–6.

111 Musifiky Mwanasali, 'The View from Below', in Mats Berdal and David Malone (eds), *Greed and Grievance: Economic Agendas in Civil War* (Boulder, CO: Lynne Rienner, 2000), p. 139.

112 James Cockayne and Daniel Pfister, 'Peace Operations and Organised Crime', Geneva Centre for Security Policy/International Peace Institute Report, 2008, p. 7.

113 For those assumptions, see 'UN Convention Against Transnational Organized Crime', UN General Assembly Resolution 55/25, 15 November 2000.

114 Cockayne and Pfister, 'Peace Operations and Organised Crime', pp. 4 and 17–18.

115 'Haiti: Security and the Reintegration of the State', International Crisis Group, Latin America/Caribbean Briefing no. 12, 30 October 2006, pp. 6–7; Williams, 'Organized Crime and Corruption in Iraq', pp. 126–8; and private communication.

116 UN General Assembly, 'Report of the High Level Panel on Threats, Challenges and Change', A/59/565, 2 December 2004, paragraph 169.

117 Private communication. The combination of globalisation and the collapse of communism creating perfect conditions for the growth of organised crime is a central theme of Misha Glenny, *McMafia: Crime Without Frontiers* (London: Bodley Head, 2008).

118 Peter Andreas, 'The Clandestine Political Economy of War and Peace in Bosnia', *International Studies Quarterly*, vol. 48, 2004, p. 29.

119 Michael Pugh, 'Rubbing Salt Into War Wounds: Shadow Economies and Peacebuilding in Bosnia and Kosovo', *Problems of Post-Communism*, May–June 2004 (special issue), p. 54; Radoslava Stefanova, 'Fighting Organised Crime in a UN Protectorate: Difficult, Possible, Necessary', *Southeast European and Black Sea Studies*, vol. 4, no. 2, May 2004, pp. 259–69; and private communication.

120 UN Office on Drugs and Crime, 'Transnational Organized Crime in the West African Region', pp. 26 and 30.

121 See Marko Hajdinjak, 'Smuggling in Southeast Europe: The Yugoslav Wars and the Development of Regional Criminal Networks in the Balkans', Center for the Study of Democracy, 2002; Thomas Köppel and Agnes Székely, 'Transnational Organised Crime and Conflict in the Balkans', in Mats Berdal and Monica Serrano (eds), *Business as Usual? Transnational Organised Crime and International Security* (Boulder, CO: Lynne Rienner, June 2002), pp. 129–40.

122 Mark Bishop, Jon Shilland, Rob Wintercross, 'Key Drug Routes for Cocaine, Heroin and the Precursor Chemicals Used in Their Manufacture: A UK Perspective', unpublished paper, King's College London, 18 March 2009, p. 10.

123 UN Office on Drugs and Crime, 'Crime and its Impact on the Balkans and Affected Countries', March 2008, p. 11.

124 Andreas, 'Criminalized Legacies of War: The Clandestine Political Economy of the Western Balkans',

Problems of Post-Communism, May–June 2004 (special issue), p. 3.

125 Roy Godson, 'Transnational Crime, Corruption and Security', in Michael Brown (ed.), *Grave New World* (Washington DC: Georgetown University Press, 2003), p. 260. The murder in March 2003 of Serbian Prime Minister Zoran Djindić indicated just how close and violent those links can become.

126 Bishop, Shilland, Wintercross, 'Key Drug Routes for Cocaine, Heroin and the Precursor Chemicals Used in Their Manufacture: A UK Perspective', p. 17.

127 Antonio L. Mazzitelli, 'Transnational Organised Crime in West Africa', *International Affairs*, vol. 83, no. 6, November 2007, p. 1,074.

128 UN, 'Final Report of the Panel of Experts on the Illegal Exploitation of Natural Resources and Other Forms of Wealth in the Democratic Republic of Congo', S/2002/1146, 16 October 2002, p. 33.

129 See Cockayne, 'Transnational Organised Crime: Multilateral Responses to a Rising Threat', International Peace Academy, Coping with Crisis Working Paper, April 2007, p. 7, fn. 46. According to one senior law-enforcement official with experience in post-conflict settings, where there is 'lack of financial regulation, oversight and management, combined ... with a prevalent traditional, underground banking system, aid money can [also] be an accelerant to corruption'. This has clearly been the case in both Iraq and Afghanistan. Private communication.

130 Glenny, *McMafia: Crime Without Frontiers*, p. 55.

131 'Haiti: Security and the Reintegration of the State', p. 5.

132 Private communication.

133 UN Office on Drugs and Crime, 'Transnational Organized Crime in the West African Region', p. 19; UN Office on Drugs and Crime, 'Cocaine Trafficking in West Africa', 2007, p. 11.

134 Private communication. Bout was eventually arrested in Bangkok in 2008. For a profile, see 'Flying Anything to Anybody', *Economist*, 20 December 2008.

135 UN Office on Drugs and Crime, 'Crime and its Impact on the Balkans and Affected Countries', p. 48.

136 *Ibid.*

137 'Organised Crime in Bulgaria: Markets and Trends', Center for the Study of Democracy, 2007, p. 14. A number of post-communist countries in Eastern Europe have passed so-called 'lustration laws' designed to remove from their posts officials who had been members of, or had collaborated with, the communist security services. The scope of these laws (and the controversy they have provoked) has varied from country to country.

138 UN Office on Drugs and Crime, 'Crime and its Impact on the Balkans and Affected Countries', p. 49. See also Center for the Study of Democracy, 'Partners in Crime: The Risks of Symbiosis Between the Security Sector and Organised Crime in Southeast Europe', 2007, pp. 1–13.

139 UN Security Council, 'Report of the Panel of Experts on Violations of Security Council Sanctions Against UNITA', S/2000/203, 10 March 2000. This report specifically draws attention to the role of Ukrainian and Bulgarian nationals, but also alludes to the role of Russian and Belarusian actors in supplying arms to UNITA.

140 For a survey of how the role of arms brokers and trafficking agents changed

after the end of the Cold War, in part as a result of the 'privatisation' of security services and the new opportunities offered by globalisation, see Brian Wood and Johan Peleman, 'The Arms Fixers: Controlling the Brokers and Shipping Agents', International Peace Research Institute, 1999; and, more recently, Hugh Griffiths and Mark Bromley, 'Air Transport and Destabilising Commodity Flows', SIPRI Policy Paper 24, May 2009.

141 For a detailed analysis of the relationship between the wars of Yugoslav succession and the rise of regionwide criminal networks, see Hajdinjak, 'Smuggling in Southeast Europe: The Yugoslav Wars and the Development of Regional Criminal Networks in the Balkans'.

142 Private communication.

143 Private communication.

144 These are well laid out in Cockayne and Pfister, 'Peace Operations and Organised Crime', p. 16.

145 Phil Williams and John T. Picarelli, 'Combating Organized Crime in Armed Conflict', in Karen Ballentine and Heiko Nitzschke, *Profiting from Peace: Managing the Resource Dimensions of Civil War* (Boulder, CO: Lynne Rienner, 2005), p. 12.

146 *Ibid.*, p. 12.

147 Cockayne and Pfister, 'Peace Operations and Organised Crime', p. 17.

148 *Ibid.*, p. 17.

149 Andreas, 'The Clandestine Political Economy of War and Peace in Bosnia', p. 31; interviews with peacekeepers returning from operations in Kosovo, Würzburg, Germany, 2000.

150 I am indebted to James Cockayne for sharing his insights on this important point.

151 Bishop, Shilland, Wintercross, 'Key Drug Routes for Cocaine, Heroin and the Precursor Chemicals Used in Their Manufacture: A UK Perspective', p. 16.

152 Cockayne and Pfister, 'Peace Operations and Organised Crime', p. 18.

153 Williams and Picarelli, 'Combating Organized Crime in Armed Conflict', p. 127.

154 Private communication.

155 James Cockayne and Adam Lupel, 'Introduction', *International Peacekeeping* (special issue), vol. 16, no. 1, 2009, pp. 4–19. See also the 'Conclusion' in the same issue.

156 Stephen Ellis, 'Interpreting Violence: Reflections on West African Wars', in Neil L. Whitehead (ed.), *Violence* (Santa Fe, NM: School of American Research Press, 2004), p. 109.

157 Nadje Al-Ali, 'The Perils of Forgetting History', *Survival*, vol. 50, no. 3, 2008, p. 151.

158 Paul Richards, 'New War: An Ethnographic Approach', in Richards (ed.), *No War, No Peace: An Anthropology of Contemporary Armed Conflicts* (Athens, OH: Ohio University Press, 2005) p. 11.

159 Neil Whitehead, 'Terrorism, Ethnic Conflict and the Culture of Violence', *Communiqué*, vol. 11, Spring 2002. For a fuller exploration of the notion that 'violent practice might be integral or fundamental to cultural practice', see essays in Whitehead (ed.), *Violence*. See also Ellis, 'Violence and History: A Response to Thandika Mkandawari', *Journal of Modern African Studies*, vol. 41, no. 3, 2003, pp. 457–75.

160 Ellis, 'Interpreting Violence: Reflections on West African Wars', p. 120.

161 Luis Martinez, *The Algerian Civil War* (London: Hurst and Co., 2000), pp. 7–14.

162 Angelina S. Godoy, 'Lynchings and the Democratisation of Terror in Postwar Guatemala: Implications for Human Rights', *Human Rights Quarterly*, vol. 24, 2002, p. 658.

163 *Ibid.*, p. 648.

164 Richards, 'New War: An Ethnographic Approach', p. 14.

165 Tripp, *A History of Iraq* (Cambridge: Cambridge University Press, 2000), pp. 6–7.

166 Nzongola-Ntalaja, *The Congo From Leopold to Kabila: A People's History*, p. 156.

167 Zoë Marriage, 'Flip-flop Rebel, Dollar Soldier: Demobilisation in the Democratic Republic of Congo', in Berdal and Ucko (eds), *Reintegrating Armed Groups After Conflict: Politics, Violence and Transition*, p. 122.

168 Christopher Browning, *Ordinary Men* (New York: Harper Collins, 1998).

169 Kieran Mitton, 'A Comparative Analysis of Approaches to Understanding Violence in Civil Conflict', unpublished MRes dissertation, King's College London, 2008.

170 Michael Burleigh, 'The Realm of Shadows: Recent Writing on the Holocaust', in Burleigh, *Ethics and Extermination: Reflections on the Nazi Genocide* (Cambridge: Cambridge University Press, 1997), p. 203.

171 Pugh, Cooper and Goodhand, *War Economies in a Regional Context*, p. 97.

172 Robert D. Kaplan, 'The Coming Anarchy', *Atlantic Monthly*, February 1994, p. 46.

173 See David Keen, *The Economic Functions of Violence in Civil Wars*, Adelphi Paper 320 (Oxford: Oxford University Press for the IISS, 1998), p. 32; Berdal and Malone (eds), *Greed and Grievance: Economic Agendas in Civil War*; and Karen Ballentine and Jake Sherman (eds), *The Political Economy of Armed Conflict: Beyond Greed and Grievance* (Boulder, CO: Lynne Rienner, 2003).

174 Ballentine, 'Introduction', in Ballentine and Sherman (eds), *The Political Economy of Armed Conflict: Beyond Greed and Grievance*, p. 1. It should however be stressed that while the increase in combatant self-financing is indeed a feature some post-Cold War conflicts, the view that conflict economies generally simply transitioned from 'patronage to self-financing' after the Cold War is too crude and requires important qualifications. See Achim Wennmann, 'Conflict Financing and the Recurrence of Intra-state Conflict', PhD dissertation, University of Geneva, June 2007, pp. 85–8.

175 Paul Collier, 'Doing Well out of War', in Berdal and Malone (eds), *Greed and Grievance: Economic Agendas in Civil War*, p. 96. For the issues involved in the 'greed and grievance' debate see Berdal, 'Beyond Greed and Grievance – and not too soon...'.

176 Collier, 'The Economic Causes of Civil Conflict and Their Implications for Policy', in *Turbulent Peace: The Challenges of Managing International Conflict* (Washington DC: United States Institute of Peace Press, 2001), p. 146.

177 Collier, 'Doing Well out of War', p. 110.

178 See Charlie Cater, 'The Political Economy of Conflict and UN Intervention: Rethinking the Critical Cases of Africa', in Ballentine and Sherman (eds), *The Political Economy of Armed Conflict: Beyond Greed and Grievance*, pp. 19–47.

179 Collier, 'Doing Well out of War', pp. 91 and 96.

180 See in particular Laurie Nathan, '"The Frightful Inadequacy of Most of the

Statistics": A Critique of Collier and Hoeffler on Causes of Civil War', *Track Two*, vol. 12, no. 5, December 2005, Centre for Conflict Resolution. See also Astri Suhrke, S. Woodward, E. Villanger, 'Economic Aid to Post-Conflict Countries: A Methodological Critique of Collier and Hoeffler', *Conflict, Security and Development*, vol. 5, no. 3, 2005, pp. 329–63.

[181] Abhijit Banerjee, Angus Deaton, Nora Lustig, Ken Rogoff, 'An Evaluation of World Bank Research, 1998–2005', 24 September 2006, p. 64, available at http://siteresources.worldbank.org/DEC/Resources/84797-1109362238001/726454-1164121166494/RESEARCH-EVALUATION-2006-Main-Report.pdf.

[182] Donald P. Green and Ian Shapiro, *Pathologies of Rational Choice Theory: A Critique of Applications in Political Science* (New Haven, CT: Yale University Press, 1994), p. 33.

[183] Nathan, '"The Frightful Inadequacy of Most Statistics": A Critique of Collier and Hoeffler on Causes of Civil Wars', p. 2. For a sophisticated critique of rational-choice theories of conflict, emphasising how they 'typically lay waste to specificity and contingency … [and] violate the complexity of individual motivation, razing the individual (and key groups) down to monolithic maximising agents', see Chris Cramer, 'Homo Economicus Goes to War: Methodological Individualism, Rational Choice and the Political Economy of War', *World Development*, vol. 30, no. 11, 2002, p. 1,846.

[184] In the 2003 World Bank report 'Breaking the Conflict Trap', Collier and his team of researchers acknowledge as much. 'While … greed cannot be entirely discounted', the report notes, 'it does not appear to be the powerful force behind rebellion that economic theorists have assumed'. 'Breaking the Conflict Trap: Civil War and Development Policy', World Bank Policy Research Report, May 2003, p. 64.

[185] Ballentine, 'Reconsidering the Economic Dynamics of Armed Conflict', in Ballentine and Sherman (eds), *The Political Economy of Armed Conflict: Beyond Greed and Grievance*, p. 260.

[186] Malone and Nitzschke, 'Economic Agendas in Civil Wars: What We Know, What We Need to Know', World Institute for Development Economics Research, Discussion Paper no. 2005/07, 2005, p. 6.

[187] Keen, *The Economic Functions of Violence in Civil Wars*, p. 32.

[188] Berdal and Keen, 'Violence and Economic Agendas in Civil Wars: Some Policy Implications', *Millennium: Journal of International Studies*, vol. 26, no. 3, 1997, p. 797.

[189] Stephen Jackson, 'Making a Killing: Criminality and Coping in the Kivu War Economy', *African Review of Political Economy*, vol. 29, no. 93/94, 2002, p. 527.

[190] Timothy Raeymaekers, 'The Power of Protection: Governance and Transborder Trade on the Congo–Ugandan Frontier', PhD dissertation, University of Ghent, 2006, p. 192. This study shows in compelling detail how violent conflict, while costly and destructive in many ways, can also produce new 'social orders' and a degree of 'governance' at the local level in the absence of properly functioning state institutions.

[191] See Jackson, 'Protecting Livelihoods in Violent Economies', in Ballentine and Nitzschke (eds), *Profiting from Peace:*

Managing the Resource Dimensions of Civil War, pp. 160–5. A corresponding distinction has been drawn between 'combat', 'shadow' and 'coping' war economies. Pugh, Cooper and Goodhand, *War Economies in a Regional Context*, pp. 8–9.

192 The term 'elite networks' is used by the 2002 UN Panel of Experts in its report on the illegal exploitation of natural resources from the DRC to denote the groups of people who active benefit from war. UN, 'Final Report of the Panel of Experts on the Illegal Exploitation of Natural Resources and Other Forms of Wealth in the Democratic Republic of Congo', p. 6.

193 For the role of transnational resource corporations and their often intimate links to war economies – a subject that remains under-researched – see Cater, 'Corporations, Resources and War: Angola 1992–2002', D.Phil. dissertation, University of Oxford, 2008.

194 I discuss these tendencies in greater detail in Berdal, 'How "New" are "New Wars"? Global Economic Change and the Study of Civil War', *Global Governance*, vol. 9, no. 3, 2003, pp. 483–9.

195 Abiodun Alao, *Natural Resources and Conflict in Africa: The Tragedy of Endowment* (Rochester: University of Rochester Press, 2007), p. 7.

196 Douglas MacArthur quoted in Fred Iklé, *Every War Must End*, 2nd revised edition (New York: Columbia University Press, 2005), p. 1.

197 Keen, *The Economic Functions of Violence in Civil Wars*, p. 12. For a similar conclusion drawn with specific regard to the DRC between 1998 and 2002, see Ingrid Samset, 'Conflict of Interests or Interest in Conflict? Diamonds and War in the DRC', *African Review of Political Economy*, vol. 29, no. 93/94, September/December 2002, p. 477.

198 Jackson, 'Making a Killing: Criminality and Coping in the Kivu War Economy', p. 528.

199 Anthony Clayton, *Frontiersmen: Warfare in Africa Since 1950* (London: UCL Press, 1999), p. 195.

200 'The Kivus: The Forgotten Crucible of the Congo Conflict', International Crisis Group Africa Report no. 56, 24 January 2003, p. 7. See also the MONUC effort to map different armed groups in the DRC in response to a request from the Security Council in 2002. UN Security Council, 'First Assessment of Armed Groups Operating in the DRC', S/2002/341, 5 April 2002.

201 'Congo: Bringing Peace to North Kivu', International Crisis Group Report no. 133, 31 October 2007, p. 27; Steven Spittaels and Filip Hilgert, 'Mapping Conflict Motives: Eastern DRC', IPIS/Fatal Transactions report, March 2008.

202 Laurent Kabila, whose career as a rebel operating in the east of the country went back to the early 1960s, was assassinated in January 2001. He was succeeded by his son, Joseph Kabila, who has served as president ever since.

203 UN Security Council Resolution 1279, 30 November 1999. In addition to the DRC, the regional signatories to the 1999 July ceasefire were Zimbabwe, Namibia, Angola, Rwanda and Uganda.

204 Spittaels and Hilgert, 'Mapping Conflict Motives: Eastern DRC', p. 24.

205 Private communication.

206 Koen Vlassenroot and Timothy Raeymaekers, 'Briefing: Kivu's Intractable Security Conundrum', *African Affairs*, vol. 108, no. 432, July 2009. pp. 1–10; 'DR Congo: Massive Increase

in Attacks on Civilians', Human Rights Watch, 2 July 2009, http://www.hrw.org/en/news/2009/07/02/dr-congo-massive-increase-attacks-civilians. According to the UN, reporting in June 2009, 1.7 million people are displaced in the eastern DRC. UN Security Council, 'Twenty-Eighth Report of the Secretary-General on the UN Mission in the DRC', S/2009/335, 30 June 2009, paragraph 23.

207 See International Rescue Committee, 'Special Report: Congo', http://www.theirc.org/special-reports/special-report-congo for the relevant documents.

208 Jackson, 'Making a Killing: Criminality and Coping in the Kivu War Economy', p. 528.

209 Ibid.

210 UN, 'Final Report of the Panel of Experts on the Illegal Exploitation of Natural Resources and Other Forms of Wealth in the Democratic Republic of Congo', p. 5.

211 Private communication.

212 'Special Report on Bisiye Mine', MONUC Kinshasa Natural Resources and Human Rights Unit, April 2008.

213 Ibid.

214 The report, which was based on fieldwork undertaken in late March 2008, focused on the southern part of North Kivu known as 'Petit Nord' (specifically the territories of Walikale, Masisi, Rutshuru, Nyiragongo and Goma). 'Natural Resource Economy in North Kivu', Report of Joint Military Analysis Cell (JMAC) and Human Rights (Natural Resources and Human Rights Unit), MONUC Kinshasa, no date. The top five resources in this region in terms of monetary value – gold, timber, wolfram, cassiterite and charcoal – give an indication of the range and diversity of resources exploited.

215 Ibid. My emphases.

216 For a detailed discussion of the relationship between war and the distinctive characteristics of natural resources, see Philippe Le Billon, Fuelling War: Natural Resources and Armed Conflict, Adelphi Paper 373 (Abingdon: Routledge for the IISS, 2005), pp. 31–50.

217 These are now organised into the FDLR, which was formed in 2000 out of the Armée de Libération du Rwanda, which consisted of ex-Rwandan Armed Forces soldiers and members of the interahamwe. According to Spittaels and Hilgert, 'a powerful core group of the FDLR movement still consists of Hutus implicated in the 1994 genocide'. Spittaels and Hilgert, 'Mapping Conflict Motives: Eastern DRC', p. 8. For a profile of the movement that stands accused of some of the worst atrocities and human-rights violations in the DRC, see Chris McGreal, 'Genocide's Children: The New Hutu Generation Raised to Kill', Guardian, 16 May 2008, pp. 8–11.

218 Raeymaekers, 'The Power of Protection: Governance and Transborder Trade on the Congo-Ugandan Frontier', pp. 95–104.

219 A justly celebrated effort to account for these many 'layers of explanations' and their interaction has now been provided by Gérard Prunier in Africa's World War: Congo, the Rwandan Genocide, and the Making of a Continental Catastrophe.

220 Vlassenroot and Raeymaekers, 'The Formation of Centres of Profit, Power and Protection: Conflict and Social Transformation in Eastern DR Congo', University of Copenhagen

Centre of African Studies, occasional paper, January 2005, p. 5. See also Michael Nest, 'The Political Economy of the Congo War', in Michael Nest, with François Grignon and Emizet Kisangani, *The Democratic Republic of Congo: Economic Dimension of War and Peace* (Boulder, CO: Lynne Rienner, 2006), p. 54.

[221] Tripp, 'After Saddam', p. 26. It was precisely the 'networks of the "shadow" state', Tripp notes, that benefited from the sanctions on Saddam's Iraq in the 1990s.

[222] For a discussion of these dangers see Keen, 'Incentives and Disincentives for Violence', in Berdal and Malone (eds), *Greed and Grievance: Economic Agendas in Civil War*, pp. 19–41.

[223] See Tripp, 'Militias, Vigilantes, Death Squads', p. 30; Andreas, 'Criminalising Consequences of Sanctions: Embargo Busting and Its Legacy', *International*

Studies Quarterly, vol. 49, no. 23, 2005, pp. 335–60.

[224] Jackson, 'Protecting Livelihoods in Violent Economies', pp. 153–4.

[225] Cockayne, 'Winning Haiti's Protection Competition: Organized Crime and Peace Operations Past, Present and Future', *International Peacekeeping* (special issue), vol. 16, no. 1, 2009, pp. 82–3.

[226] Ballentine, 'Program on Economic Agendas in Civil Wars: Final Report', p. 6.

[227] *Ibid.* See also Ballentine, 'Peace Before Profit: The Challenges of Governance', in Ballentine and Nitzschke, *Profiting from Peace: Managing the Resource Dimensions of Civil War*, pp. 447–84.

[228] Woodward, 'Do the Root Causes of Civil War Matter?', p. 155.

[229] Raeymaekers, 'Sharing the Spoils: the Reinvigoration of Congo's Political System', *Politorbis*, no. 42, 1/2007, p. 28.

[230] *Ibid.*

Chapter Two

[1] Synnott, 'The Coalition Provisional Authority in Southern Iraq', p. 5.

[2] *Ibid.*

[3] Mayall (ed.), *The New Interventionism 1991–94*.

[4] Ian Hurd, 'Legitimacy and Authority in International Politics', *International Organization*, vol. 53, no. 2, 1999, p. 381.

[5] *Ibid.*, p. 387.

[6] *Ibid.*

[7] See James Fallows, 'Why Iraq Has No Army', *Atlantic Monthly*, December 2005 and, especially, Thomas E. Ricks, *Fiasco* (London: Allen Lane, 2006).

[8] Fallows, 'Why Iraq Has No Army', p. 9.

[9] *Ibid.*

[10] Dodge, Testimony to the US Senate Committee on Foreign Relations, 20 April 2004, p. 15, http://foreign. senate.gov/testimony/2004/ DodgeTestimony040420.pdf.

[11] Béatrice Pouligny, *Peace Operations Seen from Below* (London: Hurst & Co., 2006), p. 180.

[12] Mats Berdal and Michael Leifer, 'Cambodia', in Berdal and Economides (eds), *United Nations Interventionism, 1991–2004*, pp. 58–9.

[13] Adebajo, *Liberia's Civil War: Nigeria, ECOMOG and Regional Security in West*

Africa (Boulder, CO: Lynne Rienner, 2002), pp. 173–4.

14 UN, 'Letter from the Secretary-General to the President of the General Assembly', A/59/710, 24 March 2005.

15 See Jean-Marie Guéhenno, UN Department of Peacekeeping Operations, letter to Human Rights Watch, 1 August 2007.

16 For the classic treatment of the 'spoiler' challenge in peace implementation, see Stephen John Stedman, 'Spoiler Problems in Peace Processes', *International Security*, vol. 22, no. 2, 1997, pp. 5–53.

17 United Nations, 'Report of the Panel on United Nations Peace Operations', p. x. This was also one of the chief lessons enshrined in the 'capstone doctrine' adopted by the UN's Department of Peacekeeping Operations in 2008. UN Department of Peacekeeping Operations, 'UN Peacekeeping Operations: Principles and Guidelines'.

18 For example, by making use of strategic deployment stocks, rapid deployment teams and the authority to draw on funds *before* the Security Council formally approves a mission and its budget (the so-called 'pre-mandate commitment authority' proposed by the Brahimi panel), deployments have been speeded up and some of the procurement problems that usually bedevil the start-up phase of UN missions has been partially mitigated. For the benefits of these reforms, see UN Department of Peacekeeping Operations Peacekeeping Best Practices Unit, 'Lessons Learned Study on the Start-Up Phase of the UN Mission in Liberia', April 2004.

19 United Nations, 'Report of the Panel on United Nations Peace Operations', p. 10.

20 Brian Urquhart, 'Some Thoughts on Sierra Leone', *New York Review of Books*, vol. 47, no. 10, 15 June 2000. For background on the fragility of the Lomé accord see Chapter 1, pp. 35 and 37. For a concise and persuasive account of its unravelling, see Keen, *Conflict and Collusion in Sierra Leone* (Oxford: James Currey, 2005), pp. 253–66.

21 Guéhenno, 'On the Challenges and Achievements of Reforming UN Peace Operations', *International Peacekeeping*, vol. 9, no. 2, 2002, pp. 76–7. For immediate background to the 'May crisis', see UN, 'Report of the Secretary-General on the UN Mission in Sierra Leone', S/2000/455, 19 May 2000, pp. 8–12.

22 UN, 'Report of the Secretary-General on the UN Mission in Sierra Leone', p. 1.

23 Urquhart, 'Some Thoughts on Sierra Leone'.

24 David J. Richards, 'Operation Palliser', *Journal of Royal Artillery*, vol. 127, no. 2, Autumn 2000, p. 10. Richards became chief of the general staff in 2009.

25 *Ibid.*, p. 12.

26 *Ibid.*, p. 13.

27 *Ibid.*

28 *Ibid.*

29 UN, 'Report of the Secretary-General on the UN Mission in Sierra Leone', p. 10.

30 *Ibid.* The UN's head of peacekeeping operations at the time, Jean-Marie Guéhenno, similarly acknowledged that 'the intervention of UK forces in the immediate aftermath of the crisis was critical'. See Guéhenno, 'On the Challenges and Achievements of Reforming UN Peace Operations', p. 76.

31 Keen, *Conflict and Collusion in Sierra Leone*, p. 222.

32 Anton La Guardia, 'Indian Troops to Pull out of Sierra Leone', *Daily Telegraph*, 22 September 2000; private communication. India was at the time the second-largest troop contributor to UNAMSIL and was also providing the force with its key command elements.

33 Hew Strachan, 'Making Strategy: Military–Civilian Relations after Iraq', *Survival*, vol. 48, no. 3, 2006, p. 75.

34 Keen, *Conflict and Collusion in Sierra Leone*, pp. 268–9; private communication.

35 Keen, *Conflict and Collusion in Sierra Leone*, pp. 268–9.

36 Alao and Ero, 'Cut Short for Taking Short Cuts: The Lomé Peace Agreement on Sierra Leone', p. 126.

37 Olonisakin, *Peacekeeping in Sierra Leone: The Story of UNAMSIL*, pp. 94–5.

38 Mitton, 'Rearmament, Remobilisation and Disintegration in Sierra Leone', p. 14.

39 *Ibid.* and UN Security Council, 'Second Report of the Secretary-General on the United Nations Integrated Peacebuilding Office in Sierra Leone'.

40 UN Office on Drugs and Crime, 'Transnational Organized Crime in the West African Region'; Mazzitelli, 'Transnational Organised Crime in West Africa'; Tom Cargill, 'Sierra Leone a Year After Elections: Still in the Balance', Chatham House Briefing Paper, September 2008, p. 4; private communication.

41 The Pretoria agreement of December 2002 was part of the 'Inter-Congolese Dialogue', which culminated in the peace accord signed in Sun City in April 2003. Sun City formally endorsed the Pretoria agreement.

42 Prunier, *Africa's World War: Congo, the Rwandan Genocide, and the Making of a Continental Catastrophe*, p. 277.

43 UN, 'Second Special Report of the Secretary-General on the UN Mission in the DRC', S/2003/566, 27 May 2003, pp. 3–5; private communication.

44 UN, 'Letter from the Secretary-General to the President of Security Council', S/2003/574, 15 May 2003.

45 UN Security Council Resolution 1484, 30 May 2003.

46 *Ibid.*

47 The Ituri Brigade was established as part of the expansion of MONUC authorised by the Security Council at the end of July 2003. See UN Security Council Resolution 1493, 28 July 2003.

48 See 'Operation Artemis: The Lessons of the Interim Emergency Multinational Force', UN Department of Peacekeeping, Best Practices Unit, Military Division, October 2004, p. 16.

49 Ståle Ulriksen, Catriona Gourlay and Catriona Mace, 'Operation *Artemis*: The Shape of Things to Come?', *International Peacekeeping*, vol. 11, no. 3, 2004, pp. 518–19; see also Henri Boshoff, 'Overview of MONUC's Military Strategy and Concept of Operation', in Mark Malan and João Gomes Porto, *Challenges of Peace Implementation: The UN Mission in the DRC* (Pretoria: Institute for Security Studies, 2004), p. 141.

50 'Operation Artemis: The Lessons of the Interim Emergency Multinational Force', p. 13.

51 UN, 'Report of the Secretary-General on MONUC', S/2003, 17 November 2003, pp. 18–19.

52 Ulriksen, Gourlay and Mace, 'Operation *Artemis*: The Shape of Things to Come?', pp. 522–3.

53 For those mainly interested in the development of the European Security and Defence Policy and the intramural debates surrounding it, the conclusion

that *Artemis* was a success appears to have been almost exclusively drawn from the fact that the mission showed that the EU was able to mount an operation on its own. This is not a measure of success with which this study (nor, presumably, the people of the DRC) is concerned.

54 'Supplement to an Agenda for Peace: Aide-Mémoire by France', Annex to Letter from Permanent Representative of France to UN Secretary-General dated 18 January 1996, General Assembly/ Security Council, A/50/869-S/1996/71, 30 January 1996. For a discussion of French ideas and the notion of 'active impartiality', see Berdal, 'Lessons Not Learned: The Use of Force in "Peace Operations" in the 1990s', *International Peacekeeping*, vol. 7, no. 4, 2000, pp. 55–74.

55 Unsurprisingly, given the principles of traditional peacekeeping, this mindset tended to encourage a reactive, expressly non-threatening stance to the point of viewing a peacekeeping force's vulnerability almost as a virtue in itself.

56 Joshua Marks, 'The Pitfalls of Action and Inaction: Civilian Protection in MONUC's Peacekeeping Operations', in 'Conflict Prevention and the "Responsibility to Protect" in Africa?', special issue of *African Security Review*, vol. 16, no. 3, 2007, p. 69.

57 Maciek Hawrylak and David Malone, 'Haiti, Again! A Tough Peacebuilding Task', *Policy Options*, September 2005, p. 36.

58 Alpha Sow, 'Achievements of the Interim Emergency Multinational Force and Future Scenarios', in Malan and Gomes Porto (eds), *Challenges of Peace Implementation: The UN Mission in the DRC*, p. 211.

59 'Operation Artemis: The Lessons of the Interim Emergency Multinational Force', p. 14. See also Christopher S. Chivvis, 'Preserving Hope in the DRC', *Survival*, vol. 49, no. 2, 2007, p. 28.

60 UN Security Council Resolution 1493, 28 July 2003, paragraph 26.

61 Private communication.

62 Patrick Cammaert quoted in Marks, 'The Pitfalls of Action and Inaction: Civilian Protection in MONUC's Peacekeeping Operations', p. 75.

63 'Congo: Bringing Peace to North Kivu', International Crisis Group, Africa Report no. 133, 31 October 2007, p. 13.

64 *Ibid.*, p. 14.

65 Marks, 'The Pitfalls of Action and Inaction: Civilian Protection in MONUC's Peacekeeping Operations', p. 77. See also Spittaels and Hilgert, 'Mapping Conflict Motives: Eastern DRC', p. 12. As noted in Chapter 1, the FARDC has also been deeply involved in the illegal exploitation of natural resources.

66 Marks, 'The Pitfalls of Action and Inaction: Civilian Protection in MONUC's Peacekeeping Operations', p. 77–8.

67 John Prendergast and Noel Atama, 'Eastern Congo: An Action Plan to End the World's Deadliest War', Enough! Project Report, 16 July 2009, p. 2, http://www.enoughproject.org/publications/eastern-congo-action-plan-end-worlds-deadliest-war.

68 'DRC: Massive Increase in Attacks on Civilians', Human Rights Watch, 2 July 2009, http://www.hrw.org/en/news/2009/07/02/dr-congo-massive-increase-attacks-civilians; private communication. See also 'MONUC Responds to Concerns over FDLR Reprisals', MONUC Office of Spokesperson press release, 18 July 2009.

69 Private communication.

70 UN, 'Civilians Have Paid High Price in Campaign to Integrate Congolese Armed Forces, Dismantle Foreign Ones, Special Representative Tells Security Council', Security Council press release, SC/9701, 10 July 2009.

71 Vlassenroot and Raeymaekers, 'Briefing: Kivu's Intractable Security Conundrum', p. 2. Prendergast and Atama similarly stress how 'the Congolese government often promotes insecurity and lawlessness' to advance its own predatory aims. See Prendergast and Atama, 'Eastern Congo: An Action Plan to End the World's Deadliest War', p. 1.

72 Vlassenroot and Raeymaekers, 'Briefing: Kivu's Intractable Security Conundrum', p. 1.

73 UN, 'Report of the Secretary-General on MONUC', S/2003, 17 November 2003, p. 2.

74 'Operation Artemis: The Lessons of the Interim Emergency Multinational Force', p. 14.

75 These forces can only be deployed in response to a unanimous decision of the EU Council of Ministers.

76 Ian Traynor, 'UK Blocking European Congo Force', *Guardian*, 12 December 2008; 'EU Split on Congo Troop Mission', BBC News, 8 December 2008, http://news.bbc.co.uk/1/hi/world/africa/7770916.stm. The two battlegroups on standby in December 2008 were led by the UK and Germany.

77 UN Security Council Resolution 940, 31 July 1994.

78 Malone and Einsiedel, 'Haiti', p. 185. This book chapter provides a concise and persuasive, if depressing, account of ten lost years of peacebuilding in Haiti.

79 Cockayne, 'Winning Haiti's Protection Competition: Organized Crime and Peace Operations Past, Present and Future', p. 83.

80 *Ibid.*, pp. 79–83. For a thoughtful and detailed analysis of the unsuccessful attempts to reform Haiti's public-security sector after 1994, see Johanna Mendelson-Forman, 'Security Sector Reform in Haiti', *International Peacekeeping*, vol. 13, no. 1, 2006, pp. 14–27.

81 'Haiti: Country Programme', UN DDR Resource Centre, http://www.unddr.org/countryprogrammes.php?c=80#challenges; for an overview of armed groups see also 'Haiti: Security and the Reintegration of the State', pp. 4–7.

82 Michael Dziedzic and Robert M. Perito, 'Haiti: Confronting the Gangs of Port-au-Prince', United States Institute for Peace, Special Report no. 208, September 2008, p. 4.

83 UN Security Council, 'Report of the Secretary-General on the UN Stabilization Mission in Haiti', S/2007/503, 22 August 2007, paragraph 22.

84 'Consolidating Stability in Haiti', International Crisis Group Latin America/Caribbean Report no. 21, 18 July 2007, p. 1.

85 'Haitian Leaders Resort to UN in Fighting Gangs', *International Herald Tribune*, 9 February 2007. See also 'Consolidating Stability in Haiti', pp. 2–3.

86 Private communication. Some NGOs and human-rights groups have accused the Brazilian military leadership of MINUSTAH of adopting the same brutal police tactics in Haiti as they used in the *favelas* of Rio de Janeiro and São Paulo. See also Andrew Buncombe,

'Civilians Caught in Cross-fire in Port-au-Prince Raids', *Independent*, 2 February 2007.

[87] UN Security Council, 'Report of the Secretary-General on the UN Stabilization Mission in Haiti', S/2007/503, 22 August 2007, paragraph 22.

[88] Cockayne, 'Winning Haiti's Protection Competition: Organized Crime and Peace Operations Past, Present and Future', p. 87.

[89] UN Security Council, 'Report of the Secretary-General on the UN Stabilization Mission in Haiti', S/2007/503, 22 August 2007, paragraphs 22 and 23. See also Lourdes Garcia-Navarro, 'Violence-Plagued Haiti Sees More Peaceful Days', on *All Things Considered*, NPR, 1 August 2007, http://www.npr.org/templates/story/story.php?storyId=12424369.

[90] 'Consolidating Stability in Haiti', p. 23.

[91] Dziedzic and Perito, 'Haiti: Confronting the Gangs of Port-au-Prince', p. 6.

[92] UN Security Council, 'Report of the Secretary-General on the UN Stabilization Mission in Haiti', S/2009/129, 6 March 2009, paragraph 23.

[93] Dziedzic and Perito, 'Haiti: Confronting the Gangs of Port-au-Prince', p. 6.

[94] Ulriksen, Gourlay and Mace, 'Operation *Artemis*: The Shape of Things to Come?', p. 522.

[95] For more on the crucial importance of intelligence in such environments, see Patrick Cammaert, 'Foreword', in David Carment and Martin Rudner (eds), *Peacekeeping Intelligence: New Players, Extended Boundaries* (Abingdon: Routledge, 2006), pp. xix–xxvi.

[96] Since 2000, the UK's Department for International Development has spent some $500 million 'in support of a vast range of reconstructive, institution-building and developmental projects' in Sierra Leone. Cargill, 'Sierra Leone a Year After Elections: Still in the Balance', p. 7.

[97] Urquhart, 'Some Thoughts on Sierra Leone'.

[98] Rupert Smith, 'The Use of Force in Intervention Operations', seminar presentation to the IISS, 1994.

[99] Menkhaus, 'Somalia: Governance versus Statebuilding', in Charles Call (ed.), *Building States to Build Peace*, p. 189. For the argument that the emphasis on 'power-sharing agreements for the sake of "peace"' has created a perverse incentive structure leading to more violence in the Africa, see Denis M. Tull and Andreas Mehler, 'The Hidden Costs of Power-Sharing: Reproducing Insurgent Violence in Africa', *African Affairs*, vol. 104, no. 416, July 2005, pp. 375–96. For a recognition and thoughtful discussion of the importance of focusing on the 'local level' and 'local structures' in contrast to 'the Western-style paradigm of state-building' that is 'preoccupied with forming a national executive, legislature, and judiciary', see Jarat Chopra and Tanja Hohe, 'Participatory Intervention', *Global Governance*, vol. 10, no. 3, 2004, pp. 289–305.

[100] Chesterman, Ignatieff, Thakur, 'Introduction', in Chesterman, Ignatieff, Thakur (eds), *Making States Work: State Failure and the Crisis of Governance*, p. 6; and Saikal, 'Afghanistan's Weak State and Strong Society', in *ibid.*, pp. 193–209.

[101] Bernhard Helander, 'Civilians, Security and Social Services in North-East Somalia', in Richards (ed.), *No War, No Peace: An Anthropology of Contemporary Armed Conflicts*, p. 195.

[102] 'The Role of Economic Instruments in Ending Conflict: Priorities and Constraints', report on IISS roundtable, 6 May 2009, p. 9.

[103] Peter D. Little, *Somalia: Economy Without State* (James Currey: Oxford, 2003), p. 167.

[104] George F. Kennan, *At a Century's Ending: Reflections 1982–85* (New York: W.W. Norton & Company, 1996), p. 295.

[105] *Ibid.*

[106] Menkhaus, 'Somalia: Governance versus Statebuilding', p. 187.

[107] Menkhaus, *Somalia: State Collapse and the Threat of Terrorism*, pp. 19–20; see also Little, *Somalia: Economy Without State*; and Mark Bradbury, *Becoming Somaliland* (Oxford: James Currey, 2008).

[108] Menkhaus, 'Somalia: Governance versus Statebuilding', p. 200. Lewis and Mayall similarly highlight how 'relative peace and stability has come to the two northern provinces of the former Somali Republic'. See Lewis and Mayall, 'Somalia', p. 137.

[109] Menkhaus, 'Somalia: Governance versus Statebuilding', p. 193.

[110] *Ibid.*

[111] Bryden, 'Disarming Somalia: Lessons in Stabilization from a Collapsed State', pp. 11–12.

[112] *Ibid.*

[113] Lewis and Mayall, 'Somalia', p. 137.

[114] *Ibid.*

[115] Little, *Somalia: Economy Without State*, p. 162.

[116] Menkhaus, 'Governance without Government in Somalia', p. 75.

[117] Richards, 'New War: An Ethnographic Approach', pp. 14 and 19.

[118] Synnott, 'The Coalition Provisional Authority in Southern Iraq', p. 13.

[119] See 'Iraq: Can Local Governance Save Central Government?', International Crisis Group Middle East Report, no. 33, 27 October 2007.

[120] George Packer, *The Assassins' Gate: America in Iraq* (London: Faber & Faber, 2006), p. 297. For the conflict between 'the objectives of local government reform – autonomy, local accountability [and] improvement of services' and efforts to re-establish central government in Iraq, see also Allawi, *The Occupation of Iraq: Winning the War, Losing the Peace*, p. 119.

[121] Menkhaus, 'Governance without Government in Somalia', p. 77.

[122] Marriage, 'Flip-flop Rebel, Dollar Soldier: Demobilisation in the Democratic Republic of Congo', p. 122.

[123] Matt Bryden, 'Disarming Somalia: Lessons in Stabilization from a Collapsed State', unpublished paper for project on 'Conflict, Security and Development', King's College London, March 2009.

[124] Woodward, 'Economic Priorities for Peace Implementation', International Peace Academy Policy Paper on Peace Implementation, October 2002, p. 5. An extended version of the paper appears as 'Economic Priorities for Successful Peace Implementation' in Stephen John Stedman, Donald Rothchild and Elizabeth M. Cousens, *Ending Civil Wars: The Implementation of Peace Agreements* (Boulder, CO: Lynne Rienner, 2002), pp. 183–214.

[125] For an early and incisive recognition and treatment of this problem, see de Soto and del Castillo, 'Obstacles to Peacebuilding', *Foreign Policy*, no. 94, Spring 1994. For ways of addressing it, and some recognition of the problem by the international financial institutions themselves, see James K. Boyce, 'The International

Financial Institutions: Post-conflict Reconstruction and Peacebuilding Capacities', unpublished paper prepared for Center on International Cooperation, New York University for a seminar on 'Strengthening the UN's Capacity on Civilian Crisis Management', Copenhagen, 8–9 June 2004.

[126] 'Kosovo Unemployment a "Time Bomb" Warns Analyst', Agence France-Presse, 16 October 2005, http://www.reliefweb.int/rw/RWB.NSF/db900SID/KHII-6H94FG.

[127] Michael E. O'Hanlon and Jason H. Campbell, 'Iraq Index: Tracking Variables of Reconstruction and Security in Post-Saddam Iraq', Brookings Institution, p. 40, viewed 9 July 2009, http://www.brookings.edu/saban/~/media/Files/Centers/Saban/Iraq Index/index.pdf.

[128] Morten Bøås and Anne Hatløy, 'Getting in, Getting Out: Militia Membership and Prospects for Re-integration in Post-war Liberia', *Journal of Modern African Studies*, vol. 46, no. 1, 2008, p. 34.

[129] On 23 May 2003, 'Coalition Provisional Authority Order Number 2' disbanded the Iraqi army without pay and with immediate effect. See 'Coalition Provisional Authority Order No. 2, Dissolution of Entities', 23 May 2003, available at http://www.cpa-iraq.org/regulations/20030823_CPAORD_2_Dissolution_of_Entities_with_Annex_A.pdf.

[130] According to Toby Dodge, the dissolution of the army combined with 'root-and-branch de-Ba'athification contributed to the personal, face-to-face organisation of the insurgency by putting an estimated 750,000 people out of work'. Dodge, *Iraq's Future: The Aftermath of Regime Change*, p. 15.

[131] Eric Herring and Glen Rangwala, *Iraq in Fragments: The Occupation and its Legacy* (London: Hurst & Company, 2006), p. 74.

[132] UN, 'Report of the Secretary-General on the Question Concerning Haiti', S/1995/47, 1995, p. 6.

[133] *Ibid.*

[134] *Ibid.*, pp. 6–7.

[135] Power, *Chasing the Flame: Sergio Vieira de Mello and the Fight to Save the World*, pp. 312–13.

[136] Packer, *The Assassins' Gate: America in Iraq*, p. 225.

[137] *Ibid.*

[138] In his account of the Coalition Provisional Authority's reign in southern Iraq, Hilary Synnott writes: 'People constantly told us, and I had no doubt that they genuinely believed, that the Coalition ought immediately to make life better for ordinary Iraqis: the prosperity and technological advances of our own countries showed that we had the capability; and we clearly had the resources.' Synnott, *Bad Days in Basra*, p. 206.

[139] 'Hard Lessons: The Iraq Reconstruction Experience', Office of the Special Inspector General for Iraq Reconstruction, US government publication, February 2009, p. 144.

[140] For an analysis of the failure to meet expectations with regard to water, electricity and employment in Iraq, see Herring and Rangwala, *Iraq in Fragments: The Occupation and its Legacy*, pp. 66–81. For comparisons between estimated pre-war levels of electricity generated in Iraq and the post-war period, including May 2009, see O'Hanlon and Campbell, 'Iraq Index: Tracking Variables of Reconstruction and Security in Post-Saddam Iraq'.

141 Hawrylak and Malone, 'Haiti, Again! A Tough Peacebuilding Task', p. 34.

142 Kingston Reif, 'Iraq Health Update: Conflict Fuels Iraqi Health Crisis', People's Health Movement, 5 September 2006, http://www.phmovement.org/cms/en/node/257.

143 The problems with excessive reliance on 'output metrics' are acknowledged by the US Inspector General for Iraq Reconstruction in 'Hard Lessons: The Iraq Reconstruction Experience', p. 144.

144 Quoted in Reif, 'Iraq Health Update: Conflict Fuels Iraqi Health Crisis', p. 6.

145 Synnott, *Bad Days in Basra*, p. 211.

146 'Post-Conflict Economic Recovery: Enabling Local Ingenuity', UNDP Bureau for Crisis Prevention and Recovery, Crisis Prevention and Recovery Report 2008, p. 15.

147 'Health Service Delivery in Post-Conflict States', report of the High-Level Forum on Health MDGs, Paris, 14–15 December 2005, p. 5, http://www.hlfhealthmdgs.org/Documents/HealthServiceDelivery.pdf.

Chapter Three

1 Secretary-General Kofi Annan, 'Address to the General Assembly', 23 September 2003.

2 UN General Assembly, '2005 World Summit Outcome', A/60/L.1, 15 September 2005 (henceforth 'Outcome Document'). For the last-minute negotiations leading up to the summit and its near-failure, see James Traub, *The Best Intentions* (London: Bloomsbury, 2006), pp. 381–95.

3 'A More Secure World – Our Shared Responsibility: Report of the High-Level Panel on Threats, Challenges and Change', A/59/565, 2 December 2004. For a critical, though fundamentally sympathetic, assessment of 'A More Secure World' and the work of the High-Level Panel, see Berdal, 'Reconciling the Irreconcilable?', in *Behind the Headlines*, vol. 62, no. 2, 2005, pp. 1–7.

4 See UN Security Council Resolution 1645, 20 December 2005, S/Res/1645; 'Report of the Peacebuilding Commission on its First Session', A/62/137-S/2007/458, 25 July 2007.

5 'Report of the Peacebuilding Commission on its First Session', Annex V.

6 'Outcome Document', paragraph 97.

7 'Report of the Peacebuilding Commission on its First Session', paragraph 32.

8 'A More Secure World – Our Shared Responsibility: Report of the High-Level Panel on Threats, Challenges and Change', paragraph 264.

9 For the enabling resolution creating the PBC, see UN Security Council Resolution 1645, 20 December 2005, S/Res/1645, para. 2(a).

10 UN Department of Peacekeeping Operations, 'Monthly Summary of Military and Police Contribution to United Nations Operations', accessible from http://www.un.org/Depts/dpko/dpko/contributors/index.shtml.

11 United Nations, 'Report of the Panel on United Nations Peace Operations', paragraphs 10–14.

12 For a useful and more analytical overview of the subject, see Chandra Lekha Sriram and Karin Wermester (eds), *From Promise to Practice: Strengthening UN Capacities for the Prevention of Violent Conflict* (Boulder, CO: Lynne Rienner, 2003).

13 See, for example, the Swedish government's persistent advocacy and promotion of 'structural conflict prevention'. 'Preventing Violent Conflict – A Swedish Action Plan', *UN Info*, no. 5:1, 1999; and private communication.

14 'A More Secure World – Our Shared Responsibility: Report of the High-Level Panel on Threats, Challenges and Change', paragraph 264.

15 *Ibid.*, paragraph 267.

16 The need for a 'permanent capacity' to provide strategic-level coordination was also recognised by the Brahimi Panel, though it made no specific suggestion for remedying the deficiency. See United Nations, 'Report of the Panel on United Nations Peace Operations', paragraph 47(d).

17 Martin Barber, 'Humanitarian Crises and Peace Operations: A Personal View of UN Reforms During Kofi Annan's First Term', *Journal of Conflict, Security and Development*, vol. 9, no. 3, 2009, p. 389.

18 'Delivering as One: Report of the Secretary-General's High-Level Panel on UN System-wide Coherence', 9 November 2006, paragraph 10.

19 *Ibid.*

20 'Report of the Secretary-General on the Work of the Organization 1998', A/53/1, paragraph 65.

21 NATO's operation in Afghanistan since 2003 has, notwithstanding the many communiqués stressing commonality of purpose and unity of effort, been marked by underlying tensions among allies over the strategic direction and priorities of the Alliance in the country.

22 Patrick and Brown, *Greater than the Sum of its Parts? Assessing 'Whole of Government' Approaches to Fragile States*, p. 10. Even where there is 'underlying consensus', tensions and disagreements between departments on operational matters often bedevil implementation on the ground. See for example criticism from Brigadier David Richards, commander of UK forces in Sierra Leone at the time, of the Ministry of Defence, the Department for International Development and the Foreign Office over their 'evident differences of opinion' during *Operation Palliser* in May 2000. D.J. Richards, 'Operation Palliser', *Journal of the Royal Artillery*, vol. 127, no. 2, Autumn 2000, p. 15.

23 Patrick and Brown, *Greater than the Sum of its Parts? Assessing 'Whole of Government' Approaches to Fragile States*, p. 9.

24 Stuart Gordon, 'Pursuing Joined-Up Government: The MOD's "Comprehensive Approach": A New Philosopher's Stone?', *World Defence Systems*, vol. 1, 2009, p. 163.

25 *Ibid.*

26 *Ibid.*, pp. 164–5.

27 *Ibid.*, p. 165.

28 *Ibid.*, p. 166. As for the 'pools' of funding – the Africa Conflict Prevention Pool and the Global Prevention Pool – they have, as Patrick and Brown make clear, proved at best a qualified success, with the latter in particular prone to being 'raided by other departments, particularly the FCO and the MoD, which seek flexible, unallocated funds to finance pressing contingencies'.

Patrick and Brown, *Greater than the Sum of its Parts? Assessing 'Whole of Government' Approaches to Fragile States,* p. 23; private communication.

29 Theo Farrell and Stuart Gordon, 'COIN Machine: The British Military in Afghanistan', *RUSI Journal,* June 2009.

30 *Ibid.,* and Bensahel, 'Organising for Nation-Building', p. 49.

31 Private communication.

32 See the thoughtful and informative overview of the difficulties and attempts made since 2004–05 to tackle them in Bensahel, 'Organising for Nation-Building', pp. 43–76. In the British case, relations among the three relevant departments probably reached a nadir in connection with the Iraq conflict, during both the preparations for the invasion and the subsequent post-invasion activities in the south of the country. See Synnott, *Bad Days in Basra,* especially pp. 131–49.

33 Patrick and Brown, *Greater than the Sum of its Parts? Assessing 'Whole of Government' Approaches to Fragile States,* p. 10. For a detailed assessment and generally candid recognition of the profound inadequacies of the United States' inter-agency process for supporting 'overseas contingency operations', see Office of the Special Inspector General for Iraq Reconstruction, 'Hard Lessons: The Iraq Reconstruction Experience'. See also 'Special Inspector General for Iraq Reconstruction: Quarterly Report to the US Congress', 30 April 2009.

34 Bensahel, 'Organising for State-Building', pp. 61–2. In fact, as Bensahel recalls, relations are so poorly defined that the Commission has sued the Council in the European Court of Justice in a challenge to 'the role of security policy in what it considers

to be development activities'. See also Per M. Norheim-Martinsen, 'Matching Ambition with Institutional Innovation: the EU's Comprehensive Approach and Civil–Military Organisation', Norwegian Defence Research Establishment Report, FFI-rapport 2009/01311, 3 July 2009.

35 For more on this point, see Pouligny, 'Civil Society and Post-Conflict Peacebuilding: Ambiguities of International Programmes Aimed at Building "New" Societies', *Security Dialogue,* vol. 36, no. 4, 2005. See also Pouligny, *Peace Operations Seen from Below,* pp. 67–81.

36 Pouligny, 'Civil Society and Post-Conflict Peacebuilding: Ambiguities of International Programmes Aimed at Building "New" Societies', p. 496.

37 This problem was clearly set out, with suggestions for how it might be resolved, by the Brahimi Panel in its section on 'Logistics Support, the Procurement Process and Expenditure Management'. See United Nations, 'Report of the Panel on United Nations Peace Operations', paragraphs 151–69.

38 The ACABQ is a subsidiary organ of the General Assembly responsible for scrutinising budgets submitted by the secretary-general.

39 Thant Myint-U and Amy Scott, *The UN Secretariat: A Brief History, 1945–2006* (New York: International Peace Academy, 2007), p. 15.

40 'Putting Decisions into Practice: How Will the UN Peacebuilding Commission Fulfil its Mandate?', Report on Wilton Park Conference WPS06/2, 9–10 February 2006, p. 2.

41 'A More Secure World – Our Shared Responsibility: Report of the High-Level Panel on Threats, Challenges and Change', paragraph 228.

42 'Report of the Peacebuilding Commission on its First Session', paragraph 29.

43 'Discussion Paper on HLP Recommendation to Establish a PBC', prepared by the Center on International Cooperation for a 17 January 2005 meeting hosted by the governments of Denmark and Tanzania (henceforth 'CIC Discussion Paper'), p. 3.

44 'CIC Discussion Paper', p. 8. The HLP itself did not provide a figure but was clearly anxious to avoid too large and unwieldy a configuration.

45 UN, 'Secretary-General Proposes Strategy for UN Reform to General Assembly', press release, SG/SM/9770, 21 March 2005.

46 'Outcome Document', paragraph 105.

47 'Putting Decisions into Practice: How Will the UN Peacebuilding Commission Fulfil its Mandate?', paragraph 8.

48 'In Larger Freedom: Towards Security, Development and Human Rights for All', Report of the Secretary-General for Decision by Heads of State and Government in September 2005, paragraph 114.

49 Ibid., paragraph 115.

50 Muchkund Dubey, 'Comments on the HLP', in 'Reforming the UN for Peace and Security: Proceedings of a Workshop to Analyze the Report of the High-Level Panel on Threats, Challenges, and Change', Yale Center for the Study of Globalization, March 2005, p. 65.

51 'A More Secure World – Our Shared Responsibility: Report of the High-Level Panel on Threats, Challenges and Change', paragraph 225.

52 Interviews with staff of the PBSO, New York, August 2007.

53 See 'Statement on Behalf of the Caucus of the Non-Aligned Movement in the Peacebuilding Commission', 10 October 2007.

54 Statement of Ambassador Stafford Neil (Jamaica), Chairman of G77, at General Assembly meeting on the recommendations of the HLP, New York, 27 January 2005, p. 2, http://www.g77.org/Speeches/012705.htm.

55 See Albrecht Schnabel and Ramesh Thakur (eds), Kosovo and the Challenge of Humanitarian Intervention (Tokyo/New York: United Nations University Press, 2000), especially essays in Part IV ('Selected International Perspectives').

56 Thakur, 'Towards a Less Imperfect World: The Gulf Between the North and South', Friedrich Ebert Stiftung Dialogue on Globalization Briefing Papers no. 4, April 2008, p. 5. Thakur's paper offers a telling and valuable insight into the strength of feeling within the global South on these and related issues, making the valid point that concerns and sentiments expressed by developing countries are often poorly understood and too often dismissed as retrograde, outmoded or irrelevant by countries in the North.

57 Dubey, 'Comments on the HLP', p. 65.

58 'In Larger Freedom', paragraph 116 (my emphasis).

59 Ibid.

60 This is very much in line with a more general and long-standing concern, voiced by the G77 in its formal response to the HLP, that the 'location of development issues within the confines of security threats and prevention strategies would lead to an undesirable alteration in the balance of responsibilities between the various organs of the system. It would contribute to increased concentration of power in the hands of the Security Council and further undermine

the role of the Economic and Social Council.' See Neil, Chairman of G77, at General Assembly meeting on the recommendations of the HLP, New York, 27 January 2005, p. 2.

61 Letter from Ambassador J. Bolton on Peacebuilding Commission, 29 August 2005, http://www.reformtheun.org/index.php?module=uploads&func=download&fileId=810. See also John Bolton, *Surrender is Not Option: Defending America at the United Nations* (New York: Threshold Editions, 2007), pp. 229–30.

62 'Outcome Document', paragraph 98.

63 Edward Luck, 'How Not to Reform the UN', *Global Governance*, vol. 11, no. 4, 2004, p. 407.

64 *Ibid.*, p. 408.

65 *Ibid.*

66 *Ibid.*

67 *Ibid.*, p. 409.

68 Mark Malloch Brown, 'Can the UN be Reformed?', speech to the annual meeting of the Academic Council on the UN System, 7 June 2007, copy at http://www.maximsnews.com/107mnunjune18markmallochbrownunitednationsreform.htm.

69 *Ibid.* The upshot has been that seemingly uncontroversial and sensible proposals (notably in the area of management) that had already been endorsed by leaders at the summit 'went down in flames at once or through less dramatic, but no less lethal, attrition over time'.

70 For more on this see Traub, *The Best Intentions*, pp. 394–5.

71 Malloch Brown, 'Can the UN be Reformed?'.

72 There is no evidence to suggest that Bolton ever departed from the views on the UN and its place in US foreign policy expressed in his article 'The Creation, Fall, Rise, and Fall of the United Nations' in Ted Carpenter (ed.), *Delusions of Grandeur: the UN and Global Intervention* (Washington DC: CATO Institute Publication, 1997). See also Bolton, *Surrender is Not an Option: Defending America at the United Nations*, Chapter 7.

73 For the proposals, see UN General Assembly, 'Integrated and Coordinated Implementation of and Follow-up to the Outcomes of the Major United Nations Conferences and Summits in the Economic, Social and Related Fields', A/60/692, 7 March 2006.

74 Laura Trevelyan, 'The UN's Management Crisis', BBC News, 4 May 2006, news.bbc.co.uk/1/hi/programmes/from_our_own_correspondent/4972490.stm.

75 'Secretary-General Proposes Strategy for UN Reform to General Assembly, Giving Equal Weight to Development, Security, Human Rights', press release, SG/SM9770, 22 March 2005.

76 Luck, 'How Not to Reform the UN', p. 409.

77 James S. Sutterlin, 'Some Thoughts – Mostly Cautionary – on the Recommendations of the HLP', in *Reforming the UN for Peace and Security*, p. 180.

78 Statement by H.R. Nirupam Sen, Permanent Mission of India to the UN, to the UN General Assembly on Agenda Item 149, New York, February 2007. This sense of drift and limited progress on substance is confirmed by the author's private communications.

79 Sen, 'Statement on the Report of the Peacebuilding Commission and the Report of the Secretary-General on the Peacebuilding Fund at the 62nd Session of the UN General Assembly', 10 October 2007, http://www.un.int/india/2007/ind1347.pdf.

80 Sen, Statement on the Report of the Peacebuilding Commission, 9 October 2008.

81 The formula for membership of the Organisational Committee eventually arrived at was: seven Security Council members (including the P5), seven members elected by ECOSOC, seven members elected by the General Assembly, five top providers of assessed and voluntary contributions to UN budgets and funds, programmes and agencies, and five top providers of civilian and military personnel to UN missions.

82 See 'The UN Peacebuilding Commission: Getting Down to Work', Quaker UN Office Briefing Papers, vol. 26, no. 3, May–July 2007.

83 Jayantha Dhanapala, address to the Royal Institute of International Affairs, London, 17 July 2006.

84 Luck, 'Power, Reform, and the Future of the UN', *Vanguardia Dossier*, no. 14, February–March 2005, p. 10.

85 'A More Secure World – Our Shared Responsibility: Report of the High-Level Panel on Threats, Challenges and Change', paragraph 241.

86 *Ibid.*

87 UN Peacebuilding Commission, 'Peacebuilding Support Office', http://www.un.org/peace/peacebuilding/pbso.shtml.

88 'Peacebuilding Commission', Special Research Report, Security Council Report, no. 3, 23 June 2006.

89 In this context, as international-relations analyst Dominik Zaum has observed, it is significant that 'some countries and other parts of the UN system have been very uneasy about engaging with the PBC'. This has notably been the case in regard to Timor Leste, where both the government and the UN peacekeep-ing mission 'fought tooth and claw to prevent Timor from being put onto the PBC agenda … fearing it might lead to a premature closure of UNMIT, and were wary of the added reporting arrangements and bureaucracy that it would have involved'. Author corre-spondence with Zaum, 3 August 2009.

90 Carolyn McAskie, 'The International Peacebuilding Challenge', the Lloyd Shaw Lecture in Public Affairs, Dalhousie University, 22 November 2007, p. 12. McAskie was succeeded by Jane Holl Lute in August 2008, though she left, after a brief spell, for a position in the Obama administration. Adding to the existing problems, this left the PBSO leaderless, some would say rudderless, at a critical time in its consolidation process. Judy Cheng-Hopkins was appointed her successor on 17 August 2009.

91 'Officials Hail "Historic" Inaugural Session of UN Peacebuilding Commission', UN News Center, 23 June 2006.

92 'Peacebuilding Commission', Security Council Report, no. 5, 17 October 2008, p. 13.

93 For a useful overview of the problems as seen from the field, see 'Command From the Saddle: Managing UN Peacebuilding Missions', Recommendations Report of the Forum on the SRSG: Shaping the UN's Role in Peace Implementation, FAFO, Oslo, January 1999, pp. 42–5.

94 'Peacebuilding Fund Terms of Reference', A/60/984, 22 August 2006.

95 'PBF Emergency Window: Guidelines', Peacebuilding Support Office, 2007. It should be added that the funds approved under the 'emergency window' to date (just over $10 million) are very modest indeed.

96 See UN Peacebuilding Fund, 'UN Peacebuilding Fund: Bridging the Gap Between Conflict and Recovery', http://www.unpbf.org/index.shtml for a detailed breakdown of pledges and commitments made.

97 'Peacebuilding Commission', Security Council Report, no. 5, 17 October 2008, p. 13.

98 See the US Department of Defense definition of 'operational level of war', available at http://usmilitary.about.com/od/glossarytermso/g/04531.htm.

99 At a meeting of the Organisational Committee in early September 2009 it was observed that 'the Commission had yet to develop its own rules of procedure and working methods which would contribute to the efficacy of its work'. See 'Peacebuilding Commission's Organisational Committee Adopts Draft Report for Third Session', UN press release, 4 September 2009.

100 Organisational Committee, Second Session, Summary Record of the Second Part of the 7th Meeting, General Assembly/Security Council, PBC/2/OC/SR.7/Add.1, 12 August 2008, p. 5.

101 'Peacebuilding Commission', Security Council Report, no. 5, 17 October 2008, p. 12.

102 Conor Cruise O'Brien, *The United Nations: Sacred Drama* (New York: Simon & Schuster, 1968), p. 14.

103 'Strengthening the strategic focus of PBF funding' was also a principal recommendation of a comprehensive donor-commissioned evaluation of the Peacebuilding Fund released in June 2009. Nicole Ball and Mariska van Beijnum, 'Review of Peacebuilding Fund', 4 June 2009, http://www.unpbf.org/docs/PBF_Review.pdf.

104 'IPI Task Forces on Strengthening Multilateral Security Capacity', report of International Peace Academy, Task Force II, June 2008.

105 UN Peacebuilding Fund, 'Priority Plan for the UN Peacebuilding Fund – Guinea–Bissau', 24 June 2008, http://www.unpbf.org/docs/PBF_Guinea_Bissau_Priority_Plan_(English_24Jun2008).pdf.

106 Private communications.

107 'Central African Republic: Anatomy of a Phantom State', International Crisis Group Report no. 136, 13 December 2007. For the priorities, see General Assembly, 'PBC Endorses Integrated Strategy for Long-Term Development', PBC/49, 6 May 2009.

108 General Assembly, 'Peacebuilding Commission CAR Configuration 3rd Meeting', PBC/49, 6 May 2009.

109 Private communication.

110 Helander, 'Civilians, Security and Social Services in North-East Somalia', p. 202.

111 'Prime Minister Datuk Seri Abdullah Ahmad Badawi, at the Opening of the Ministerial Meeting of the Nonaligned Movement Coordinating Bureau', 29 May 2006.

112 See for example the telling opening remarks by the president of the General Assembly, Miguel d'Escoto Brockmann of Nicaragua, 'At the Opening of the Thematic Dialogue of the General Assembly on the Responsibility to Protect', UN, New York, 23 July 2009, http://www0.un.org/ga/president/63/statements/openingr2p230709.shtml. See also 'Responsibility to Protect: An Idea whose Time has Come – and Gone?', *Economist*, 23 July 2009.

113 Thakur, 'Towards a Less Imperfect World: The Gulf Between the North and South', p. 2.

[114] See statements made by China and Russia in January 2007 explaining their use of the veto to prevent Security Council censure of Myanmar's military junta, and similar statements made in July 2008 when vetoing a draft resolution calling for sanctions against Zimbabwe. See also their position in the Human Rights Council's special session on Sri Lanka in May 2009. See 'Provisional Verbatim Record, Security Council, 5619 Meeting', S/PV.5619, 12 January 2007; 'China and Russia Veto Zimbabwe Sanctions', *Guardian*, 12 July 2008.

[115] S. Neil Macfarlane, 'The "R" in BRICs: is Russia an Emerging Power?', *International Affairs*, vol. 82, no. 1, 2006, p. 56.

[116] As Rana Mitter, writing in 2003, has argued: 'China signs up to the current consensus in large part on an instrumentalist basis, calculating that there are concrete and symbolic benefits to be gained from doing so, rather than from any widespread conversion to solidarist values within the policy-making classes. As long as the maintenance of a party state is paramount, there will always be a significant barrier in the way of internalisation of those values'. Rana Mitter, 'An Uneasy Engagement: Chinese Idea of Global Order and Justice in a Historical Perspective', in Foot, Gaddis and Hurrell (eds), *Order and Justice in International Relations*, p. 225.

[117] 'Kosovo's Fragile Transition', International Crisis Group Report, 25 September 2008. See also Zaum, 'Lessons from State-Building in Kosovo', Institute for Public Policy Research, September 2009.

Conclusion

[1] UN Security Council 5895th Meeting, 20 May 2008, S/PV.5895, p. 10.

[2] Bryden, correspondence with author, 15 August 2009.

[3] R. Anders Nilsson, 'Dangerous Liaisons: Why Ex-Combatants Return to Violence: Cases from the Republic of Congo and Sierra Leone', PhD dissertation, Uppsala University, 2008, p. 194.

[4] This is the particular focus of Berdal and Ucko (eds), *Reintegrating Armed Groups After Conflict: Politics, Violence and Transition*.

[5] Stephen Ellis, 'How to Rebuild Africa', *Foreign Affairs*, vol. 84, no. 5, September–October 2005.

[6] Prunier, *Africa's World War: Congo, the Rwandan Genocide, and the Making of a Continental Catastrophe*, p. xxxvi.

Adelphi books are published eight times a year by Routledge Journals, an imprint of Taylor & Francis, 4 Park Square, Milton Park, Abingdon, Oxfordshire OX14 4RN, UK.

A subscription to the institution print edition, ISSN 0567-932X, includes free access for any number of concurrent users across a local area network to the online edition, ISSN 1478-5145.

2009 Annual Adelphi Subscription Rates		
Institution	£381	$669 USD
Individual	£222	$378 USD
Online only	£361	$636 USD

Dollar rates apply to subscribers in all countries except the UK and the Republic of Ireland where the pound sterling price applies. All subscriptions are payable in advance and all rates include postage. Journals are sent by air to the USA, Canada, Mexico, India, Japan and Australasia. Subscriptions are entered on an annual basis, i.e. January to December. Payment may be made by sterling cheque, dollar cheque, international money order, National Giro, or credit card (Amex, Visa, Mastercard).

For more information, visit our website: **http://www.informaworld.com/ adelphipapers.**

For a complete and up-to-date guide to Taylor & Francis journals and books publishing programmes, and details of advertising in our journals, visit our website: **http://www.informaworld.com.**

Ordering information:
USA/Canada: Taylor & Francis Inc., Journals Department, 325 Chestnut Street, 8th Floor, Philadelphia, PA 19106, USA. **UK/Europe/Rest of World:** Routledge Journals, T&F Customer Services, T&F Informa UK Ltd., Sheepen Place, Colchester, Essex, CO3 3LP, UK.

Advertising enquiries to:
USA/Canada: The Advertising Manager, Taylor & Francis Inc., 325 Chestnut Street, 8th Floor, Philadelphia, PA 19106, USA. Tel: +1 (800) 354 1420. Fax: +1 (215) 625 2940.

UK/Europe/Rest of World: The Advertising Manager, Routledge Journals, Taylor & Francis, 4 Park Square, Milton Park, Abingdon, Oxfordshire OX14 4RN, UK. Tel: +44 (0) 20 7017 6000. Fax: +44 (0) 20 7017 6336.

The print edition of this journal is printed on ANSI conforming acid-free paper by Bell & Bain, Glasgow, UK.

1944-5571(2009)49:4;1-L